BEST TRADING STRATEGIES

Master Trading the Futures, Stocks, ETFs, Forex and Option Markets

ISBN-13: 978-1493799572

By: The Speakers of Traders World Online Expo #14

CONTENTS

Contents 2

Introduction 5

Failing Your Way to Success by Adrienne Toghraie 6

How to Trade Eminis by Steven Primo 14

How to Analyze and Profit from the Major Moves in the Markets by Steve Wheeler 24

Cutting Edge News, Social Media, & Twitter Sentiment Analytics by Bill Dennis 37

New TA Tools for Mobile Traders by George Krum 46

Algorithmic Trading with Human Interaction by Thomas Barmann 53

Machine Designed Trading Systems by Michael L. Barna 59

How to Increase Your Trading Profits with the New THD Directional Volume Indicator by Gail Mercer 73

Ninjacators Real Time Supply and Demand Indicator Intro to the Indicator Of The Month Club By Troy Epperson 81

APA Zones Exposing the Hidden Order Flow by Gabriel Brent 87

How to Predict the Closing Direction of Any Market by Scott Andrews 95

Uncomplicate Your Trading by Al McWhirr 104

Speakers of Traders World Online Expo #14

Dual Look Back Momentum Reversals with Time and Price Strategies by Robert Miner 113

The A-B-C Price Pulse – Trading the C – Wave by Jack Crooks........118

Without these 2 Important Keys, You Will Fail in Trading by Ken W. Chow 127

The Market Profile™ Graph and and How to Trade It by Tom Alexander..134

The Simplest Proven Day Trading Method with a Track Record by Gerard P. Reynaud 143

The Perfect Growth Stock by Ross Givens..146

Harmonic Wave Convergence – The New Paradigm of Currency Trading by Steve Gregor..155

A Simple Edge for Active Traders by Eloy Fenocchi 162

Trend Following Trades Addresses The Trend Traders Challenge of Trading Only Trending Markets with its Patent Pending TFT AMA by John Karnas..170

Use This 4-Step Trading Process or You May Find Yourself in a 12-Step Program By John Matteson..182

The Gartley Trading Method by Ross Beck...190

The Mystery of Interest Rate Futures and the Stars by Barry William Rosen...193

Slope and Noise – Relationship to Profit by Brady Preston..............197

World Cup Trading Championship: History and the Advantages of Competing by Chad Robbins and Mark Ayoub 209

"Edwards Angles" New Paradigm Pitchfork Trading by Byran Edwards..217

Other Kindle Books..223

On Demand Videos from the Traders World Online Expo Expires December 31st, 2013..228

Copyright..230

Disclaimer..231

Speakers of Traders World Online Expo #14

INTRODUCTION

This is one of the most fascinating books that was ever written about trading because it is written by twenty-five expert traders. These traders have many years of experience and they have learned how to turn technical analysis into profits in the markets. This is extremely difficult to do and if you have ever tried to trade the markets with technical analysis you would know what I mean. These writers have some of the best trading strategies they use and have the conviction and the discipline to act assertively and pull the buy or sell trigger regardless of pressures they have against them. They have presented these strategies at the Traders World Online Expo #14 in video presentations and in this book. Go to www.TradersWorldOnlineExpo.com

What sets these traders apart from other traders? Many think that beating the markets has something to do with discovering and using some secret formula. The traders in this book have the right attitude and many employ a combination of fundamental analysis, technical analysis principles and formulas in their best trading strategies.

Trading is one of the best ways to make a lot of money in the world if one does it right. One needs to find successful trading strategies and implement them in their own trading method. The purpose of this book is to present to you with some the best trading strategies in my opinion so that you might be able to select those that fit you best and then implement them into your own trading strategy.

I wish to express my appreciation to all the writers in this book who made the book possible. They have spent many hours of their time and hard work in writing their section of the book and the putting together their video presentation for the online expo.

Failing Your Way to Success by Adrienne Toghraie

Would you choose to do the most difficult things in the most difficult ways, while failing at every step in order to succeed?

Now, before you say, "No, why in the world would I do that?" I want you to realize that most people who become professional traders make the choice to fail their way to success. Of course, they do not make this choice knowingly, but the end result of their decisions is to take this path.

It is generally understood that the way to succeed in professions other than trading requires advanced education and degrees, plus years of training and personal development. This is not so with trading. Unfortunately, people can enter the profession of trading without this type of preparation, but they cannot succeed over time without it.

Doing it all Wrong

Several years ago, I conducted a phone consultation with a young trader named Phil. With his trust fund in hand, a knack for getting top grades without having to work hard, and a love of excitement, Phil had decided to enter the world of trading and make a killing in the markets.

Unfortunately, he soon had his first loss proving that the markets were not fair. Still, he had expected a few losses, so, he continued to trade without any hard preparation and he continued to lose. As the losses mounted and became more serious, he began to suffer the usual emotional reactions to loss: fear, insecurity, hesitancy, and inconsistency.

Phil decided to get coaching without paying for the service and called me to see if I could fix the problem. When queried about his preparation for trading, Phil brushed off the subject lightly, as though it had little relevance to his situation. Months later, he called again and was willing to listen but still unwilling to take the right action. Since Phil had never had to work hard before, he was dismayed at the level of commitment that successful trading would require of him. Here are some of the steps he took on the easy way to failing at trading:

The Hot Tip

Phil did not want to put in the required time and effort while developing his own system. Instead, he used his brainpower to come up with what he thought was an excellent idea. Why not find someone who would provide him with the right information? He started frequenting the local watering holes where traders went after hours. He met Jim who started giving him hot tips over beer and pretzel sticks. This system worked very well for three months. Then, while using one of Jim's tips, Phil lost a significant amount of money.

The Magic Guru

Then, Phil decided that he would resort to his old, standby strategy: if he could not get success for free, he would pay for it. He started with a trip to the local book warehouse that had a wall of books on every subject. For the first time, Phil was seriously reading and learning about trading. However, he was not able to put into practice all that the book instructed him to do. Once again, he lost heavily.

The Magic System

Phil resorted to paying for success once again. He decided that he needed to buy a proven system. To his credit, Phil did some fairly extensive research and purchased one of the most expensive and best-regarded systems available. What Phil wanted was a mechanical system that anyone could follow. The problem was that Phil was not just anyone and when it came down to following the rules of the system even when he thought he saw a loss or an opportunity developing, he could not follow the system. Soon, he was breaking every rule of the system and ignoring all of the signals. The result: heavy drawdowns.

It was at this point that Phil called again. Over a year and a half had passed since I had heard from him, and he was sounding less confident of himself. In fact, he was getting ready to leave trading if this last round of strategies did not pay off.

The Magic Therapy

When everything else failed, Phil decided to come to a *Trading on Target Seminar*, still without commitment on his mind. He was once again attempting to find an outside source to solve his basic trading problems. What he found at the seminar from listening to the other attendees and the material presented was that all along, he was trying to take a short-cut while only making his path longer. He decided on private consultation. When I took Phil on as a client, it was before I had the rule that a trader had to have a system or methodology that he believed would work. The only thing between Phil and his success was his own psychological sabotage.

As we began to look at Phil's personal strategies, attitudes, and beliefs, it became clear that he had stacked the deck against himself. His patterns of behavior were filled with a daily regime of self-destructive acts. He abused his health by living on junk food, getting too little exercise and sleep, and consuming too much alcohol and drugs. When he was not engaged in trading, he filled his spare time with long hours on the couch watching television or cruising the local clubs with friends attempting to pick up women. He belonged to no organizations, churches, or clubs. He had no family and no strong friendships to support him.

All of Phil's life choices were based on a set of beliefs and attitudes that were anathema to success. He believed that life was a game where you simply found the fastest and easiest strategy to win. Once he had experienced losses in the markets, he was angered and wanted revenge. Phil knew now that if he were to succeed, he would have to go back to square one and start with a plan.

Dedicated Losers

Phil's trading odyssey is by no means a unique one. Many traders employ similar strategies. If they perceive trading as a game, and not as a profession, they will attempt to play at it as opposed to working at it. Once a trader has established a mental picture of "how things are," he will unconsciously look for evidence that supports his picture of reality or create circumstances that reinforce that picture.

More of these failing strategies are:

Trading is a game, so I'll play it like one.

This was one of Phil's losing beliefs. Trading is a serious profession that makes its money from people who don't see it as one.

Trading provides on-the-job training, so I don't need to go into it completely prepared.

By the time you have learned the important lessons from the on-the-job training, you are out of the business.

I can leverage a small amount of capital into a fortune, so I don't need to be well capitalized.

Under capitalization is the single most common reason for a trader to wash out early in the game. Far too many new traders start out with $5,000 nest eggs that are rapidly consumed by the vultures.

I can buy my way to success.

Yes, it is important to have solid capital behind you, but money cannot replace commitment, research, mastery, self-discipline, emotional mastery, and time.

I do not need to practice self-discipline in my money management or in my life because I have brilliance and/or a great system and/or unlimited resources.

The term "self-discipline" conjures up images of pain, loss, or sacrifice to many people who are unable or unwilling to deal with those feelings. People who have not practiced self-discipline in their former lives will not come by it easily in their trading lives.

I can borrow the money and pay it back in no time.

Traders who borrow the money from their children's college funds, in-laws, friends, or from home equity are trading with the same odds as playing roulette in Las Vegas, because they are working with "scared money." When in a draw down, visualizations of loved ones losing the benefit of money accumulated for their future needs will keep you in a drawdown state of mind, where sabotage is king.

I can trade from anyplace.

Trading in an environment that is not conducive to trading is another shortcut that is a sure way of failing to succeed. A trader's home may have a secure and comfortable room that is completely separate from any of the demands of the home and still not allow a trader to trade from home. For example, when his trading is not going well, the temptation to visit the TV room or the kitchen or play with the children can be overwhelming.

I don't need to test my system. I know it works.

The time required to adequately test a system seems like a waste of time for a trader who has already invested a great deal of time developing it.

This psychology business is nonsense.

I'm fine. This may be one of the most common failing strategies. After spending years creating the capital necessary to trade, doing research and developing and testing a system, the average committed trader is often not interested in looking within himself for the answers to his future success.

My goal is simple: Make a lot of money.

What is wrong with this strategy? It's only a part of the answer. Yes, a trader needs to go into trading with the idea of making money. But, he needs to have a good relationship with money in the past in order to have a good one in the future. In addition, it cannot be the only goal, because a trader must enjoy the process of trading or he will create a lot of exciting and interesting ways to lose money.

How to Get Off the Failing Path

It is impossible to change the direction of a diesel train, loaded with 75 cars of cargo, plunging down the tracks at ninety miles an hour. However, it only takes one broken rail pin to derail the train and destroy the entire shipment. Turning a trader to a constructive, success path that will lead to long-term success after he has been on a misguided path without transformation of perception is equally impossible. But, destroying his trading career can be as easy as derailing that train.

Instead of waiting for your career to be permanently derailed, I have a few suggestions that can help you switch tracks without crashing. The first and most important step is for you to re-evaluate your business plan. What? You have none? Well, that does not surprise me. Traders who have completed a comprehensive business plan are, by definition, on the right track. But, they are in the great minority. A good business plan for trading requires you to confront all of the issues discussed in this article and many more.

Oh, by the way, after I got Phil to work on his trading business plan, he had a trading epiphany. He suddenly got it! Trading was a business and a profession all wrapped up in one. It wasn't a game anymore and Phil made the commitment to do what it took to succeed. Funny thing, by following his plan, life and trading became a lot easier than working to take the easy path of failing his way to success.

Conclusion

Failing your way to success is a common, but painful way to travel, especially when traders reach the dead end at full speed. Often, the most immediately successful trading strategies are losing strategies over time. For traders who have not made the full commitment to trading as a profession and have not done the planning required for long-term success, the choices will make sense at the time. They will look easy, simple, and quick, but they will seldom be the right ones. The way off of this path is doing what you should have done in the very beginning: take the time to create a complete trading business plan and succeed your way to success, instead.

For more information contact Adrienne Toghraie, Trader's Success Coach, www.TradingOnTarget.com

HOW TO TRADE EMINIS BY STEVEN PRIMO

Hello, my name is Steven Primo and I have been actively trading the markets for over 36 years now - beginning as a 9-year Specialist on the floor of the Pacific Stock Exchange, to managing a private Emini Fund. Later on in my trading career I held the position of Director of Education for a number of websites until I ultimately became the President and Founder of my own company, Specialist Trading, which focuses primarily on trading education.

I have experienced and traded just about every market environment imaginable, from the Crash of '87 to the great Bull market that followed, but I've learned that one thing remains constant. Regardless of market conditions, most traders - especially Emini traders - will blow out their accounts within the first year of trading. Please be aware that when I say "blowout" I do not mean they will sustain a series of losses. I mean they will actually lose their entire trading accounts. It's at this point that a prospective trader must make a decision - either to end his dream of one day becoming a successful trader, or to begin the long journey towards acquiring the insights, wisdom, and trading strategies needed in order to become a successful trader. The good news is that I've already made that journey for you. My goal is to shorten your learning curve by teaching you how to trade with the edges that I've already acquired within my 36 years of trading. My goal is to teach you how to trade with the Specialist's Edge.

In this article I will share with you two highly powerful but simple edges that have literally sustained me throughout my trading career.

Edge #1

Let's begin by looking at Fig. 1 and asking a simple question, "Has this ever happened to you before?" The market has been moving to the downside and continues to head lower until you decide it's bottomed out and time to buy. After all, according to your strategy the Emini looks tremendously oversold and the 5-minute bar appears it's due for a quick rally to the upside. So you jump in and buy at the market, but guess what happens? By the end of the day and into the next, the market begins to make new lows. (Fig. 2) Look familiar?

(Fig. 1)

Best Trading Strategies

(Fig. 2)

This is the way 99.9% of all traders' trade - by trying to pick tops and bottoms. But what if there were a simple tool designed to get you on the right side of the market? One that could tell you the right time to buy and the right time to sell. At Specialist trading there is. Enter the **Buy/Sell Line**, the most powerful trading tool we employ at Specialist Trading and the foundation for virtually every trading strategy we teach. If there were only one technique I could use for the remainder of my trading career, it would be this.

So just what is the **Buy/Sell Line**? It's the 50-period simple moving average, that's it. But in order to use this tool properly you must first plot the moving average and then ask yourself this question prior to each and every trade. Regardless of the strategy, regardless of the direction or time frame, always ask yourself before you pull the trigger - "Where is price in relation to the Buy/Sell Line?" You'll only come up with two possible answers: 1) if price is above the

Buy/Sell Line you'll only be taking buy signals, and 2) if price is below the Buy/Sell Line you'll only be taking sell signals. That's it. This tool is so simple but extremely powerful and has literally saved me hundreds of thousands of dollars throughout my trading career.

So how could this technique have helped us in the previous scenario? Let's take a look at the same chart but this time with the **Buy/Sell Line** added (Fig. 3) Now we ask ourselves "Where is price in relation to the Buy/Sell Line?" and we notice that price has always been below the 50-period sma. Therefore we had no business in the world originally considering going long the Emini. Had we simply followed the rule from the start and looked for shorting instead of buying opportunities, we could have easily locked in some nice gains to the downside by mid-morning.

(Fig. 3)

To see how well this tool transfers onto different time frames and in different directions, I've included snapshots of a 60-minute chart (Fig. 4), a daily chart (Fig. 5), and a 5-minute chart of the infamous "Flash Crash" of May 2010 (Fig.6). To summarize, in order to use the Buy/Sell Line properly always ask your self this question before you pull the trigger "Where is price in relation to the Buy/Sell Line?" If price is above the Buy/Sell Line you'll only be looking to go long, and if price is below the Buy/Sell Line you'll only be looking to go short. I'm confident that once you begin to employ the Buy/Sell Line properly, you will take your Emini trading to the next level.

(Fig. 4)

(Fig. 5)

(Fig. 6)

Edge #2

As I mentioned earlier, most traders attempt to buy at the exact bottom and sell at the exact top, regardless of market, time frame, or choice of trading strategy. But just where is the bottom and just where is the top? As we've all seen in the current market environment, the Eminis can go as high or low as they want, and much more than anyone could have ever expected. Rather than try to pick a top or bottom, which is often a recipe for disaster, the only thing needed is for a trader to wait for **confirmation.** This is the assurance that the Emini has concluded it's downward course and is now once again headed in an upward direction. Much like a train leaving the station for it's desired destination.

So what exactly is **confirmation**, and how do we use it? A buy *confirmation* consists of when the Emini, in an uptrend, has sold off to a satisfactory buy level and then reverses and trades higher than the *previous bar's high*. Conversely, a sell *confirmation* consists of when the Emini, in a downtrend, has risen to a satisfactory sell level and then reverses and trades lower than the *previous bar's low*. We buy and sell only on *confirmation*, regardless of the strategy used.

The chart below (Fig. 7) shows a common trading technique used by many traders - going long the Emini once the stochastic oscillator has gone into "oversold" territory ("overbought" for sells). Had we purchased the Emini at point (A), when the indicator first went below the 20 threshold and into supposed oversold territory, we would have most likely held on to a losing trade for an extended period of time?

But had we simply waited for **confirmation** at point (B), we would have entered the trade only after the future had traded one tick above the previous day's high, a signal that the Emini had begun to move in our desired direction. Ironically, this is where most traders would have "thrown in the towel" and exited their original losing position! Using this method would have saved you a lot of money, grief, and heartache. The purpose of waiting for **confirmation** is not only to get us **IN** at the beginning of a trend, but to keep us **OUT** of bad trades as well.

For more information go to: stevenprimo@specialisttrading.com, www.specialisttrading.com

(Fig. 7)

Best Trading Strategies

This edge works in any direction... (Fig. 8)

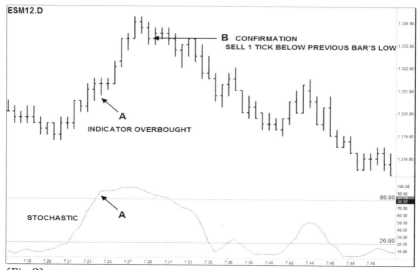

(Fig 8)

And in any time frame. (Fig. 9)

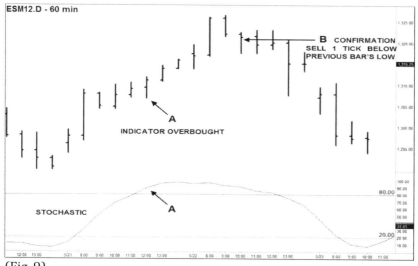

(Fig. 9)

As you can see, if one trades without using **confirmation** they are simply guessing as to where to place their buy or sell orders. This guesswork is relative to top picking and bottom fishing; styles of trading that will eventually yield negative results.

But please be advised, just because a trade has been confirmed does not guarantee that it will become profitable. But by waiting for **confirmation**, one can substantially increase the odds for a successful trade in their favor. **Confirmation** is the verification that a directional move has concluded and that the trend has once again resumed. A Specialist always waits for his trade to be confirmed before entry.

Summary

Ultimately, these edges will not guarantee that all your Emini trades will become profitable, but if you do decide to employ these tools I feel you will substantially increase your odds for success. Why? Because The **Buy/Sell Line** is designed to put you on the right side of the market whereas **Confirmation** is the verification that a directional move has concluded and that the trend has resumed. Once you learn how to fully employ both these techniques you will be trading with the Specialist's Edge.

How to Analyze and Profit from the Major Moves in the Markets by Steve Wheeler

Let me start by introducing myself. I am a full time trader and trainer in the futures markets. I run a real time trading room four hours each trading day. I have traded for over 25 years and concentrate primarily on the currency (FOREX), crude oil, gold and stock index futures markets, such as the S & P E-mini.

I have developed a full suite of charts and indicators known as the Trendicators and a market analyzer known as the TradeFinder. I have included a sample trading plan with specific trade setups.

What follows are the fundamental elements you need to be consistently profitable in the futures markets.

Making money in the market is a matter of being on the right side of the market. Specific to the futures markets, there are both up and down moves each day that provide trading opportunities. One approach to the markets is to look for evidence of major support and resistance levels based on chart history. Many people ask me which time frame that I look at for my trading, and my best answer is that I look at all of them. A good analogy would be that if you were going to buy or short a stock, you would most likely start by looking at a weekly or daily chart. Why would you approach the futures markets any differently? To put the odds in your favor, you must find things that occur over and over and trade with this information.

A Study of Price Behavior

A very predictable pattern of price behavior is that prices tend to cycle between range contraction and range expansion. Range is a measure of the difference between the high and low of a given price bar.

See chart example below for Range Contraction and Range Expansion:

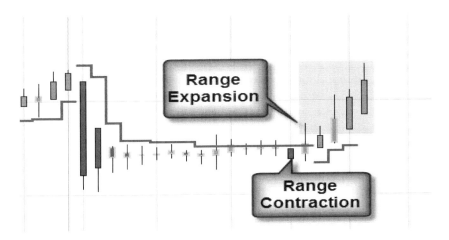

Your Preparation:

Preparation consists of market observation over a period of time so that the trader can build confidence in knowing what usually happens in the market and how to profit from the recurring market behavior that repeats itself every day.

To take advantage of cycles in the markets, observe the typical move that a market moves after it moves up or down out of a range contraction pattern.

Best Trading Strategies

The real objective is to build knowledge of probabilities of market behavior so as to take consistent profits out of specific trading instruments. The following are observations of market behavior that will help to put the probabilities in your favor

Price behavior can be summed up by knowing how to determine the overall patterns in varying time frames. See the chart example below of a move up out of a Range contraction pattern of about ten points on the S & P Futures market.

Example of a break higher after a break above range contraction:

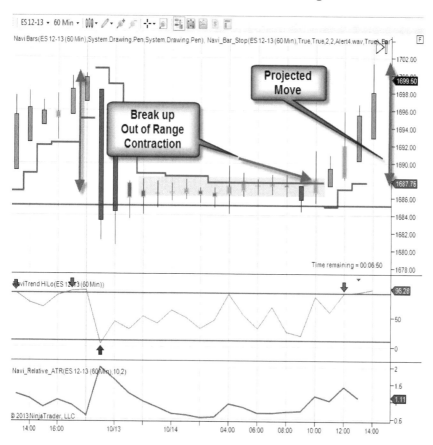

One way to determine if you have this type of pattern developing is to look at the current range relative to past range. The Navi_Relative_ATR indicator below will indicate a relatively low value when you have a range contraction setup. See chart example below:

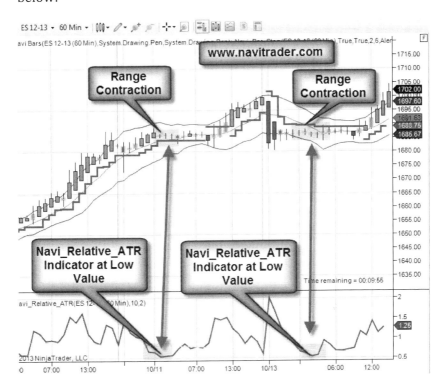

You can take advantage of this pattern of low volatility that will predict an upcoming period of higher volatility. If the market breaks down from a period of low volatility, you will likely have a down trending market. Down trends consist of lower highs and lower lows. Up trending markets consist of higher highs and higher lows. Markets move in a wave formation, and when each wave is formed, a pivot is formed. These pivots form Lower Highs and Lower Lows in a down trend, and Higher Highs and Higher Lows in an uptrend.

See Down Trend example below:

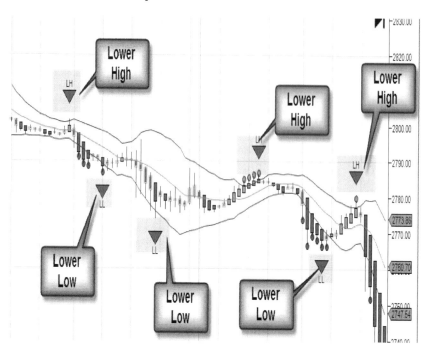

Navitrader Trendicator © chart

Velocity indicates the speed at which the market is moving. Trend indicates the overall direction of movement. If we have an extremely high velocity down moving market, then the probabilities favor a continued down move. If we have an extremely high velocity up moving market, then the probabilities favor a continued up move.

The examples below are trade setups or chart conditions that you can use to take your trading to the next level. The examples below make use of the NaviTrader Trendicator© charts. The Trendicator© charts will display a red price bar when the market is moving down and a green price bar when the market has moved higher on that specific price bar.

Examples of Trend Determination:

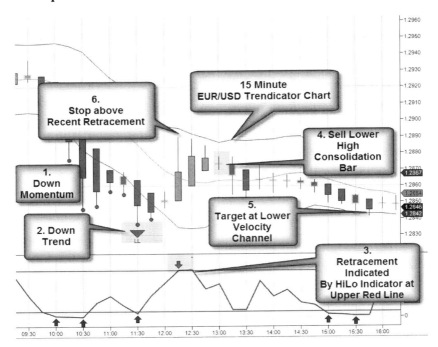

Above chart uses the Trendicator© Charts running in the NinjaTrader platform.

The above Trendicator chart shows you the current price direction for each price bar. The short trade setup above includes the following elements:

Current momentum is down indicated by the red dots on the price chart.

Price has made upside retracement based on HiLo indicator (HiLo indicator moved above 90)

Price is again moving down based on Red closing price bar color

Price target is lower velocity channel (blue line)

The long trade setup includes the following elements:

Current momentum is up indicated by the green dots on the price chart.

Price has made downside retracement based on HiLo indicator (HiLo indicator moved below 10)

Price is again moving up based on Green closing price bar color

Price target is upper velocity channel (blue line)

Swing Trading Method:

Within a trend, the momentum will sometimes change or shift, for example we may have had down momentum, and then the momentum shifts back to up momentum. This change in momentum is what I refer to as a "momentum shift". A momentum shift represents one of the best trading opportunities, because it usually accompanies the beginning of a new trend.

Look for a shift in Momentum and trade in the direction of current momentum. If the most recent momentum is down, then enter short trades. If most recent momentum is up, then enter long trades. One of the best indicators of a trend change is when we get a momentum shift. In the example below, we previously had "up" momentum and then an extreme momentum shift to the down side.

Use a momentum indicator such as the BigMo© indicator and stay short when Red Dots first appear on the screen and remain in the short trade until Green Dots appear on the screen, indicating that you now have a momentum shift in the opposite direction. The red dots indicate extreme down momentum and green dots indicate extreme up momentum.

Speakers of Traders World Online Expo #14

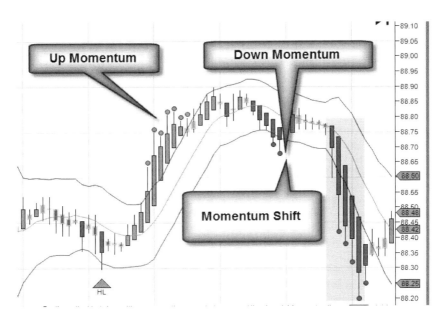

Above Red and Green dots are the NaviTrader BigMo© indicator

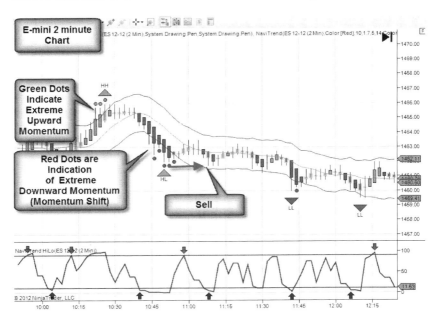

Above Red and Green dots are the NaviTrader BigMo© indicator

Risk Management

A primary downfall of beginning traders lies in not knowing how to manage risk. The use of stop losses (known as stops); is one important tool in trading futures. An even more important tool is known as position sizing. Position sizing answers the question of how many contracts should I trade in the futures markets, and how many shares should I buy or short in the stock market.

We know that trading is all about how to react to your successes as well as trades that don't go your way. No discussion of trading would be complete without a discussion of risk management. For futures trading, risk management is established with a combination of the use of stop orders combined with position sizing. You need to pair a proven strategy along with risk management. Risk management is accomplished in general by never taking a "big" loss on any one trade. I suggest that you start by making sure that on any one trade that you do not risk any more than one percent of your trading account. You will need to calculate **before** you enter a trade whether you would be risking more than one percent of your trading account.

To calculate position size you need to know some basic information such as the following:

Account Size

Risk Percentage that you are assuming

Tick value of contract you are trading

Number of ticks of your initial stop loss order

A Risk Management calculation example for the e-mini would be as follows:

Entry price = 1438.25

Initial Stop level = 1436.25 = 8 ticks on the S & P E-mini

8 ticks x tick value of $12.50 = $100 $100 x 1 contract = $100 risk on this trade.

Account Size = $10,000

In this example, you would be able to trade 1 contract $10,000 x 1% = $100 maximum risk

Like any profession, you need to be prepared to take on the markets in a structured and methodical manner. If you study the above principles, you will better understand overall market behavior and you will be equipped to begin to consistently benefit from the great opportunities that exist each day in the markets.

Platform:

As you develop your trading skills, I suggest that you use a professional trading platform that will allow you to trade directly from the charts and will allow you to trade in simulation mode as well as to execute trades in your futures account. It is important to develop you skills as to how to use your trading platform while in simulation mode so as to minimize trading errors after you are trading your actual trading account.

Below is an example of The NaviTrader Trendicator© charts and the NinjaTrader Chart Trader platform:

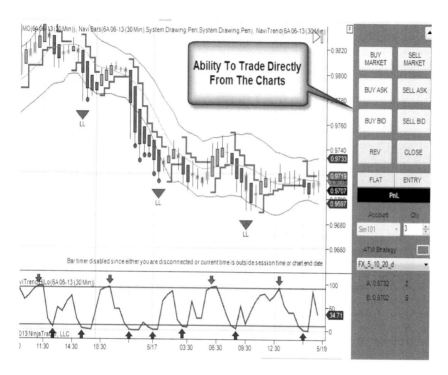

Trading in simulation mode will help you to develop your confidence and an overall methodology that fits your personality.

Fear:

Most traders will develop fear as they trade due to a history of losses. Like any fear, the way to overcome it is to face it and continue to do what you fear, while taking correct risk management precautions. An advantage of having a trading platform that provides for simulation is that you will be able to trade in simulation mode to build a plausible plan and to develop more confidence in your approach to trading. As you trade in simulation mode, develop a set of notes that will act as the beginning of your trading plan. Trade in simulation mode until you have mastered the use of the trading platform you have chosen. As you trade in simulation mode, practice developing the discipline needed to execute your trading plan. Through repetition, you will begin to develop into a polished and profitable trader

Sample Trading Plan Follows:

Trade 6E Contract between 3:30 AM Eastern and 6:30 AM Eastern

I will trade 3 contracts

For Long Trades, I will look for pullback patterns

I will review 60 Minute chart for long term Intraday Trend

I will trade consistently with Momentum on the 5 and 10 Minute charts

For Long Trades, I will wait for a pullback, defined as NaviTrend HiLo

Moving below 10 value

Buy 2 ticks above Green signal Bar

After In the Trade, I will use 5, 10 and 20 tick targets

Manage stop based on NaviBar Stop on 10 minute chart

For Short Trades, I will wait for a pullback, defined as NaviTrend HiLo

Moving above 90 value

Sell 2 ticks below Red signal Bar

After In the Trade, I will use 5, 10 and 20 tick targets

Manage stop based on NaviBar Stop on 10 minute chart

Best Trading Strategies

Please let us know if you need any help in developing your approach to profitable trading. Send an e-mail to support@navitrader.com with any questions and visit our website at www.navitrader.com

If you have any questions on the material in this publication, please send an e-mail to support@navitrader.com   www.navitrader.com

Cutting Edge News, Social Media, & Twitter Sentiment Analytics by Bill Dennis

How did EOTPRO Developments Inc. get started, and what is its product and customer focus?

EOTPRO Developments Inc. launched in 2006 as End of Trend Trading on the TradeStation Platform as an add-on provider for the retail trader. Once EOTPRO was launched we continued to build new analysis based on customer feedback. As our business grew, we expanded to include different markets and created leading edge products and services that offer high tech solutions for our clients. In 2008 and 2009 we branched out to provide analysis to other charting platforms.

Our product line and services have changed dramatically over the last few years to service more professional traders and institutional clients.

EOTPRO offers the following analytics and services:

News story and Twitter sentiment

Risk Analysis Systems

Technical Indicators

Co-location Services

Professional Programming Services

EOTPRO products and services support equities, ETFs, indices, and associated derivatives (options; futures). Forthcoming initiatives focus on foreign exchange.

Technical indicators are currently available for TradeStation, MultiCharts, NinjaTrader, E-Signal, and we will be expanding into other professional platforms.

When did you introduce your Machine Readable News offering, and how does it compliment your other products?

EOTPRO commenced beta testing of its Machine Readable News (MRN) product during the fourth quarter of 2012. It complements the product suite because the offering is a natural extension of the technical analysis tools, as it provides another piece of information to confirm/invalidate signals. It also provides the research-oriented trader/investor with new ideas that deserve further investigation.

What is Machine Readable News and social media sentiment? How does it work?

Using content from over four million websites and blogs as well as 44 news sources, EOTPRO's Machine Readable News and social media offering is the industry's most advanced service for automating the consumption and systematic analysis of news and social media sentiment for the individual trader.

Twitter volume is growing quickly and is expected to reach one billion tweets per day in the near future. EOTPRO has decided to integrate a patent pending process developed by Social Market Analytics (SMA) to distil this information. These metrics allow clients to eliminate the noise from seemingly unquantifiable chatter and uncover trading opportunities.

Hedge funds and institutional firms looking to add a new dimension of market data to their trading models currently use these types of market analytics.

There are 3 metrics available:

1. Corporate news sentiment indicators - covering 5600 US stocks

2. SMA Twitter sentiment indicators - covering approximately 3000 US stocks plus ETFs and indices

3. Major blog and internet news site sentiment indicators - covering 5600 US stocks

These 3 metrics are designed to give the trader a complete spectrum of news and social media sentiment information that can be used as new and additional information to make trading decisions for the US markets.

EOTPRO's news and social media analytics plots directional sentiment directly on the screen live as an indicator or is displayed inside a standalone web portal, this happens within sub-seconds of a news or social media release.

Traders and investors can use this new metric of information to generate high probability trading ideas and protect against portfolio drawdown.

Comprehensive analytics suite delivered several ways

EOTPRO delivers a comprehensive suite of social media and news analytics in the following ways

1. Inside our web portal, accessed via a web page

2. Inside popular trading platforms

3. API connection

Best Trading Strategies

Product use scenarios

1. Quantitative traders and analysts can quickly incorporate news and social media sentiment into their strategies and develop sentiment-based investment and trading models. API access also available.

2. Discretionary traders can support trading decisions with advanced news and social media analytics tools and indicators.

3. Fundamental investors can monitor company, sector or market sentiment in news and social media for idea generation and benchmarking.

4. Retail brokers and institutional portals can provide value-added content that attracts new clients and trade flow by generating appealing trading ideas.

5. Risk managers can better understand the potential for abnormal risk and predict volatility and negative price pressure; they can discover unknown correlations across instruments.

6. Traders or investors wishing to monitor risk in their portfolio will also find this product beneficial. For those invested in stocks and unavailable to trade intraday there is also a solution in the form of an alert system. The system alerts the user to high sentiment stories. This will provide instant real time notifications on high impact news events or social media chatter that may affect the return on a portfolio.

Idea generation via the EOTPRO Web Portal

The MRN web portal offers traders an intuitive and easy to use interface to uncover opportunities and monitor risk. The portal displays social media and news sentiment on US stocks and is targeted at discount brokers, investment advisors, hedge funds, traditional asset managers, and investment portals.

An example of an effective way to use news and social media analytics would be to focus on significant spikes in sentiment from the securities normal state.

EOTPRO can provide traders with several top and bottom lists of stocks and futures with extreme sentiment. Extreme sentiment is typically denoted with a score that traders can use to find opportunities.

The following top 10 lists highlight potential trading opportunities available:

1. Stocks with highest sentiment news stories

2. Stocks with highest blog and internet news sentiment

3. Stocks with extreme Twitter sentiment

4. Real-time news sentiment of indices and sectors

5. Real-time blog and internet sentiment of indices and sectors

6. Real-time Twitter sentiment of indices and sectors

Machine Readable News Web Portal screenshots

The screen shot below shows a depiction of the Machine Readable News stand alone web portal. This is where stocks with the highest sentiment news stories are displayed. A built in charting application is also included.

Best Trading Strategies

Index and sector sentiment

The web portal provides extremely useful information for futures and ETF traders. EOTPRO aggregates news and social media in real-time for the major indices so that traders can monitor news and social media biases and manage their trading strategies accordingly.

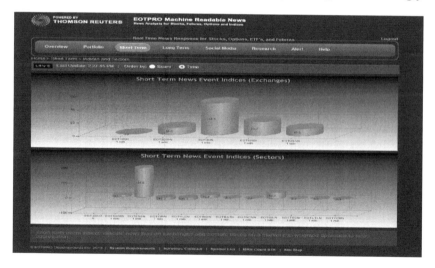

Charting for futures and index traders

News metrics can be plotted in a charting application, as seen here:

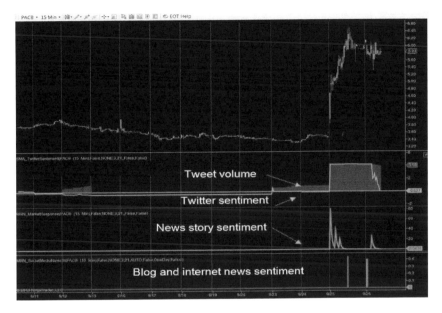

News sentiment is represented as real-time indicators so that traders can identify the most powerful market moves. This information can be viewed in two ways, a web portal and via a charting package.

API connection

EOTPRO has a sophisticated API connection with the following attributes:

1) Low latency connection with CME Aurora servers.

2) TCP/IP live data stream that maintains connection state.

3) Includes methods for historical data requests.

4) Sequenced data that allows missing data requests after any data stream interruptions.

5) Full API documentation.

6) Available through TCP/IP allowing a connection in any programming language.

7) Open source API model built for C# .NET.

Why now? Why is news and social media sentiment relevant?

News and social media impacts markets significantly. This new trading tool will assist in helping traders and investors understand when news and Twitter sentiment will move markets. The MRN data identifies when a security will behave differently and this may allow a significant edge in the marketplace. EOTPRO aims to provide clients with the most innovative data solutions and provide the edge necessary to succeed.

What resources, education and training are available?

EOTPRO's training curriculum has been designed for the beginner and professional consulting is available to the most advanced quant.

To learn more please visit us here: www.eotpro.com

Contact us at:

info@eotpro.com

sales@eotpro.com

Screen shot examples

The following example shows how a large portfolio can be displayed to monitor for news and social media sentiment risk.

The building height is represented to show news sentiment.

The building footprint is the social media sentiment.

This view shows a stock in the portfolio that has negative sentiment and may expose the portfolio to risk. Alerts are sent to the user in real time.

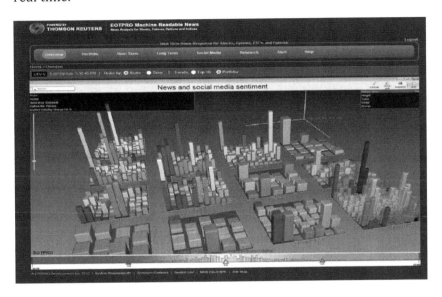

In this TSLA example below, Twitter and news sentiment both turned negative 1 hour before the pull back in the stock. This event occurred due to reports that a Tesla vehicle had caught fire.

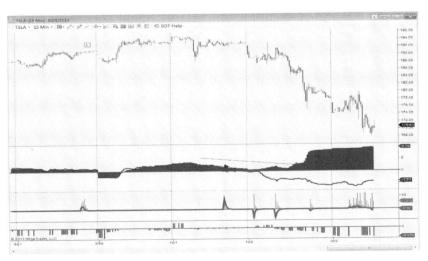

NEW TA TOOLS FOR MOBILE TRADERS BY GEORGE KRUM

In this presentation we'll briefly discuss the newest additions to the OddsTrader app family, while focusing on using the Vix as a market timing tool, and on combining pivot levels with pivot moving averages, cycles and oscillators.

USING VOLATILITY INDICES AS MARKET TIMING TOOLS

Using the Vix as a market timing tool has a long history and has many variations. With the introduction of dozens of new volatility indices by the CBOE, the same strategies can now be applied to a broader range of financial instruments.

Thanks to the newly released Vix market timing module, developed by the CIT Dates team for the Oddstrader app family, iPhone/iPad users are finally able to have this powerful tool at their fingertips.

But before we discuss the specifics of our newest TA tool, we'll provide some background information first.

The Vix (CBOE Volatility Index) was developed by the Chicago Board Options Exchange in 1993. It has since evolved into the world's premier barometer of investment sentiment and market volatility. It is calculated by using real-time SPX option bid/ask quotes for near and next-term out of the money SPX options with at least eight days left to expiration.

The Vix falls within the category of so-called "contrarian" indicators. It tends to move between well-defined ranges, which change over time. However, whenever the index reaches the top or bottom of that range, it is a reliable signal that a change in trend for the market is imminent.

When investors are running scared or feel a high degree of uncertainty about the future trend of the market, they tend to pile into put options bidding up their premium, which coincides with spikes in the Vix index. The opposite is true for bullish periods, when there is less fear, and the investing public feels less need to buy puts. Such periods coincide with lower Vix readings suggesting complacency.

By monitoring the behavior of the Vix, and using it as a gauge of investment sentiment, alert investors can position themselves ahead of the crowd and anticipate when market turns are likely to occur.

There are several ways of achieving this. The first one is to look at the actual Vix readings and try to determine when the index is about to peak or bottom. For user convenience, the module automatically highlights the high/low Vix range for the selected time period. The problem with this approach is that, although in the long run the index moves within a well-defined range, there is no telling in advance at precisely what level the reversal will take place.

The other option is to apply different technical indicators to the Vix in order to determine when it's reaching overbought/oversold levels. Systems in this group are centered around the use of the RSI, moving averages of varying length, MACD, DMI, Bollinger bands, Williams %R, etc.

We are introducing a new approach. We apply a pivot moving average (pma, discussed below) to both the Vix and the SPX, and monitor whether the indices cross/trade above/below the pma. The indices can trade either on opposite sides or on the same side of the average. Under normal conditions, one would expect the indices to trade on the opposite side of the average. When they trade on the same side of the pma, that usually is an early warning signal that the trend is about to change. From a practical point of view, however, we've noticed that rushing to react merely because the indices are suddenly trading on the same side of the average can lead to frequent whipsaws.

Therefore, we've included two signal lines in our module. The signal line at the bottom of the top chart turns green when Vix is trading below and SPX is trading above the pma. The line turns red when the opposite occurs, i.e. when Vix trades above and SPX trades below the pma. If the indices trade on the same side of the pma, the current signal remains in effect until reversed.

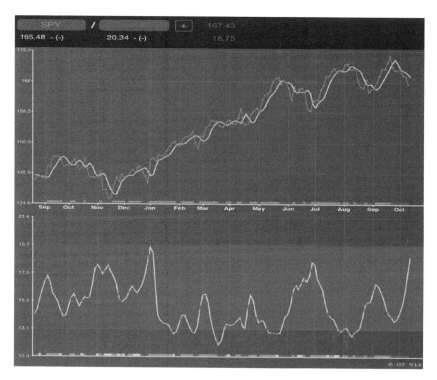

The signal line in the bottom (second) chart turns yellow when the indices trade on the same side of the pma. As explained above, this could be an early warning signal that the trend is about to change, but could lead to frequent whipsaws as well. User discretion is advised.

This approach has several advantages.

First, the pma is fixed for the day, and is clearly displayed on the chart. This gives users the ability to plan their trades ahead of time, to place alerts for predetermined index levels, etc.

Second, users are not limited to the SPX/Vix pair, but can enter other pairs of their choice, e.g. QQQ/QQV, IWM/VIX, etc. Currently the CBOE is tracking more than 20 volatility indices. Once Yahoo Finance starts reporting historical data for all of them, users will be able to monitor many more pairs.

Third, if you input a random pair of stocks, the top signal line will show when stock A outperforms stock B on a relative strength basis.

Now let's proceed with a brief case study in order to evaluate the effectiveness of such an approach.

The SPX/Vix pair gave a sell signal for the SPX on Monday, September 23rd. The NDX/QQV (QQQ/VIX, QQQ/QQV) pair remained on a buy signal until Friday, September 27th. Then both pairs remained on a sell signal, despite the spike up on Tuesday, October 1st, and the fact that the Qs made a new high. As of this writing, October 9th, the SPX has lost some 50+ points, while the NDX dropped 100+ points.

In summary, the new Vix market timing system provides users with deeper insight into the markets that cannot be achieved by traditional TA tools. Smartphone users can use this powerful new market timing tool either as a standalone signal generating system, or as an instrument to support their other analytical tools.

PIVOT LINES AND CYCLES

The second item for discussion is the OT Pivots app. Developed at the request of our users, it combines the power of pivot lines with cycles and several other new tools developed on the basis of pivot lines, in order to provide a unique perspective on stock, etf, forex and index trading.

Pivot lines are a simple but effective tool developed by floor traders in order to quickly and objectively identify intraday support/resistance levels. They can be used by range, breakout and trend traders alike, and can be used along with any other TA tool or indicator.

There are four main ways to calculate pivot points, and they are all available from the app: Standard, Woodie, Fibonacci and Camarilla.

In addition to the four pivot point calculations, the app includes our proprietary pivot moving average. It soothes out price fluctuations, defines areas of possible support and resistance, and helps visualize the trend. Changing the setting for the pma affects the frequency of the trading signals generated by the app.

The other two indicators included in the app are the Pivot oscillator, and the Cycle bars.

The Pivot oscillator helps identify overbought oversold levels, and plays a role in generating the trading signals.

The cycle bars are a dynamic cycle indicator which extracts the dominant short and medium cycles and plots them in future, alerting ahead of time for potential change in trend dates.

The pma and the Pivot oscillator are combined in such a way as to produce three sets of trading signals.

The top signals (green and red triangles) are generated on the basis of price crossing above/below the pivot moving average.

The bottom signals (green and red triangles) are generated on the basis of the pivot oscillator crossing above/below the 0 (zero) line.

The signals in the middle (green/red bar) are activated when the top and bottom signals are in agreement.

In summary, OT Pivots provides users with easy access to pivot points and several trading strategies in a very affordable package.

Two more things need to be mentioned before we conclude.

First, here's an update of the SPY seasonal chart, first published in TradersWorld #55. As of this writing at the beginning of October, the correlation of SPY with the seasonal pattern continues to be very strong at 81.87%:

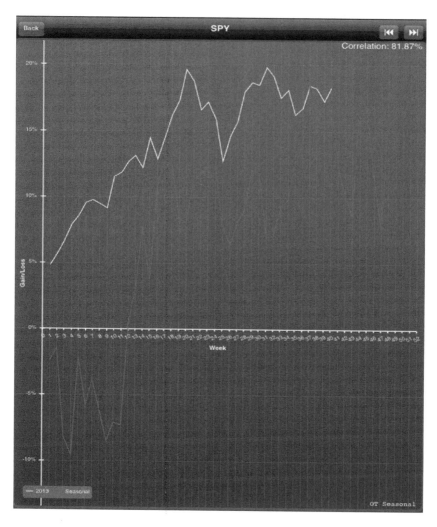

One would be hard pressed to find a more accurate forecasting tool for the first three quarters of the year; with the exception, probably, of the decennial pattern, also available with the same app.

And, second, keep your eyes open for new and exciting additions to the OddsTrader app family in the very near future.

For more information contact George Krum at www.citdates.com

Speakers of Traders World Online Expo #14

Algorithmic Trading with Human Interaction by Thomas Barmann

All financial markets: Stocks, Commodities, Currencies, and Treasuries are dominated by more than 85% on Institutional trading or investment decisions. The NeverLossTrading® specific algorithms and indicators help you to spot and trade along with institutional money moves so they happen.

Experience, how you can use our algorithmic trading or quant trading model to find high probability trade setups on multiple tick-, range-or time-frames.

How can one predict the future price of a stock or other asset?

Historically, technical analysis is used to predict a future happening on the price chart. The first technical analysis is reaching back to the 1600's, when "Japanese Candle Sticks" started their development in tracking historic price moves to predict the price moves to come. Japanese is one of the most graphical languages on the planet. The western world casually say candle sticks to the graph, which expresses a relation of the high, low, open and close of the price, painted over a period of time or contracts closed. The Japanese word for the graph is **TAKURI,** meaning "trying to gauge the depth". Another interpretation: candle sticks are the "footprints in the sand of a price move". Our days, commonly, technical analysis is used to predict a future happening on the price chart.

Times changed and we can leave the technology and analysis of the past behind us. Today's trading-platforms and computer technology allows the private investor to use complex algorithms to filter and portrait assets with potential directional price moves, putting you at par with the big investment houses of the world.

How else would you know, which of the 42,000 assets traded in the US are of institutional interest?

Latch on to today's trading world and use the leading edge technology of NeverLossTrading® to your trading/investing advantage.

The NLT-Price Move Model

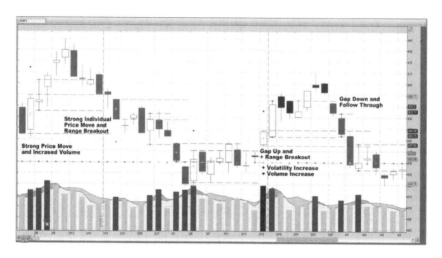

How far can price patterns be predicted?

We consider two major and conflicting theories:

Theory-1: There is a price behavior, which repeats itself

Cause and Effect – When one event causes another to happen.

The Cause is why it happened. The Effect is what happened.

Repeating Price Behavior Theories are: Head and shoulders, flag patterns, cup and handle and many others are patterns that are recorded and assumed that they repeat themselves. Our studies and documentation show that the probability of an assumed pattern to conclude is in the range of 55% - 59%.

Theory-2: The price behavior is random and cannot be predicted.

Random Price Distribution Theories often rely on a Markov chain, where the price development is random, but in the vicinity of an expected statistical price distribution.

The NeverLossTrading Algorithm or Quant Model

NeverLossTrading® considers price patterns and random price behavior, while an independent price-behavior model was developed:

Key to the NeverLossTrading® pricing model is the institutional price move, which is detected and reported by assuming "crowd behavior": Leaders initiate a price-change and followers jump on the new direction, defining our price-entry-point from where the potential future price-point in the natural distribution of prices is extrapolated and traded. The trade orientation is rather short-term: 1-5 bars, in reference to the time-, tick-, or range-unit observed: Individual price moves to the up- and downside are traded.

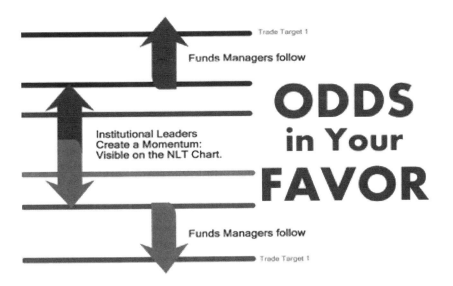

Prices accumulate prior to a price move and our indicators are identifying this stage by measuring price-, volume- and volatility development, with the NLT-specific market pressure model.

Prices **test** the **high/low** of a range prior to breakout. Again, our sensors are triggered and alarm us.

Breakout to the next price increment. It shows and is highlighted right on our charts and picked up by our scanners.

The **price breakout is noticed** by key market participants and is either:

Confirmed – **and we trade along with it.**

Not confirmed – and we stay out of the trade.

With NeverLossTrading, we built a natural behavior model, which considers repetitive action in behavior of leaders and followers: The crowed is following the leaders. With our mathematical models, we translated this into a trading plan, with defined entries and exits, where the price behavior on the chart is sectioned in:

Purple Zones: Times where a rather random price behavior with counter trade activities is expected.

Blue Zones: Dominant to Upside Price Moves

Red Zones: Where Downside Price Moves are Dominant

IBM Price Chart with Purple Zone and Breakout

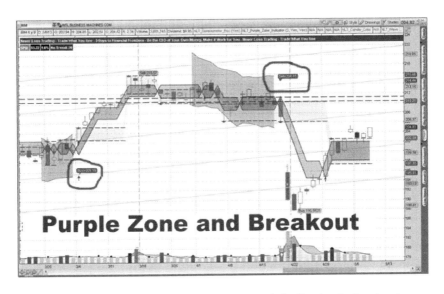

NeverLossTrading uses a proprietary model of price behavior to measure and point out high probability trade setups at institutional money flow. Here are some examples:

Strong directional moves: NLT Top-Line

Early Trend Moves: NLT Top-Line

End of Purple Zone: NLT Top-Line and NLT HF-System

Momentum/Volatility Change: NLT HF-Systems

Top & Bottom Finder: NLT HF-Systems

Continuation Patterns: TradeColors.com

Based on this model we developed multiple trading concepts, suiting the needs of day traders and swing traders. Our mentorship programs include all software installed, individual classes and coaching programs.

In addition, we launched an <u>Alert</u> service, where we are fulfilling the needs of the long-term or short-term investors and day trader.

Let modern algorithms and data-bases filter out trading opportunities for you, while you stay in the ultimate control to make the trading decision.

To be part of this, check contact@NeverLossTrading.com

Machine Designed Trading Systems by Michael L. Barna

Computers assist us in many areas of our lives ranging from casual social interactions to mathematically intense financial engineering. Algorithms perform the majority of trading now on most exchanges and this trend will continue into developing countries and their exchanges. When a trader places an order, smart order routers take over and "work" the order to various venues so as to get the trader the best fills. High Frequency Traders execute algorithms capturing expected pricing mismatches between exchanges, markets and symbols. Directional systematic traders perform detailed and exhaustive optimizations and searches exploring new potential regions of alpha. All algorithms are difficult to design and the capturing of consistent inefficiencies elusive. The chance of strategy over fit is very high, hardware or software failures a possibility and continued regulatory oversight and requirements onerous. The potential for profits, however, is so high that "any" research showing possible improvements in returns remains highly desired. However, alpha that was once easy to capture becomes far more difficult or impossible to capture sometimes just a short time later as evident by GETCO's profits sliding from $430M in 2008 to $25M as of September, 2012 and Barclays Systematic Traders Index with 466 programs and $260B under management showing historic recent declines in profitability.[1] In the financial strategy design

---

[1] http://www.zerohedge.com/news/2013-02-13/how-getco-went-hft-trading-giant-dwarf-and-raked-over-50-million-te-expenses-along-w

arena you either evolve or perish.

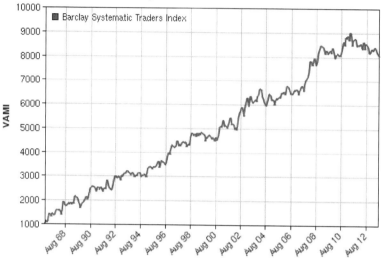

Source: BarclayHedge

With computers so much a part of our daily lives in financial markets today, and consistent trading profits so elusive, why are most algorithm developers still manually designing trading strategies? Why has the "machine" been so underutilized for machine-automatic-creation of trading algorithms? Clearly with the endless combinations of inputs, mathematical functions and optimizations possible, the trader-developer must realize that the only way to even partially cover the potential research space for alpha lies in using a machine that assists the human in the design process. Several reasons for this underutilization of CPU throughput as applied to financial engineering become evident upon research. First, software development costs are very high with estimates in the range of $28 per Source Line Of Code(SLOC)[2]. Costs to develop software compared to project hardware costs have inverted since 1955 with software costs now amounting to 90% of the total

---

[2] http://cs.iupui.edu/~mroberts/n361/SDArticle1.pdf

development costs. The "brain drain" of software developers and engineers in the U.S. is so significant that several million engineering jobs in the US remain unfilled, even with the influx of H-1B visa card holders entering the US on work visas. Wall Street firms looking to find C++ programmers, for example, not only have a very substantial security and vetting issue, they also have a lack of qualified applicants to choose from. Further evidence of this existing "software crisis" is that 99% of all possible CPU cycles are not used.[3]

Clearly a method that allows for rapid code writing combined with financial algorithm design is needed; however the overall process is non-trivial. Computational infrastructure must include trading simulation, trading implementation, machine learning tools, overall fitness or objective functionality, code language translation routines, over fit avoidance criteria, entry and exit tactics and data preparation and preprocessing. Even with such an infrastructure and development base, how would a trader or developer have any reasonable assurance that such an approach is viable, practical, and cost effective and can actually produce any long term profits?

LEARNING ALGORITHMS

Financial modeling is difficult at best and since the data is non-stationary, discontinuous, full of shocks, black swans, meltdowns and other data irregularities, a unique approach to machine learning as applied to trading strategy design must be developed. Further, this uniqueness is necessary because potential alpha lies in regions that have not been mined out due to either complexity with the mining process itself or with costs associated with accomplishing the data mining. An excellent algorithm that has a high cost to develop provides a first level barrier to entrance. Few

---

[3] http://www.tradingsystemlab.com/files/CISC%20Architectures.pdf

people will have the algorithm, so perhaps the possible alpha that could be captured may not be completely mined out yet. Indeed, a process that is difficult and costly to develop and implement might be the best place to start looking for appropriate algorithms for the difficult task ahead.

Let's start with the machine learning process[4]. Using the older traditional methods of Artificial Intelligence(AI) as applied to Machine Learning is probably not the area to focus on to find new alpha. What is needed is an algorithm that writes another algorithm, an algorithm that is fast, accurate, creates new and unique models and actually writes code.

	FAST?	ACCURATE?	WRITES CODE?	CREATE NEW MODELS?
Neural Networks	NO	YES	NO	NO
Case Based Reasoning	YES	YES	NO	NO
Classification	YES	YES	NO	NO
Regression	MAYBE	MAYBE	NO	NO
Expert Systems	MAYBE	MAYBE	NO	NO
Intelligent Agents	NO	YES	NO	NO
Genetic Algorithms	YES	YES	NO	NO
Genetic Programming	YES	YES	YES	YES

TABLE 1. Modeling Algorithms

Table 1 shows the main algorithm types that we consider for our learning algorithm selection. After a review of potential algorithms we note that Genetic Programming is fast, accurate, writes code and creates new models.

Let's impose the no free lunch (NFL) theorem in our selection of algorithms[5]. The NFL theorem states that any two optimization algorithms are essentially equivalent when they are applied over all problems. If we assume that in our difficult financial modeling

---

[4] http://en.wikipedia.org/wiki/Machine_learning
[5] http://en.wikipedia.org/wiki/No_free_lunch_theorem

problems that we require an algorithm that is good at a myriad of problems, then the selection of any specific algorithm may not be any better than another algorithm. What then falls out of our requirement list for our machine designed trading algorithm is speed, uniqueness and the ability to write code. Again, a fast Genetic Program looks like the preferred approach.

Let's look again at the speed issue. Modern many-core or hyper threading approached can produce amazing speed improvements over algorithms running on a single thread[6]. Moving lower within the CPU architecture, down to the CPU level where individual trading algorithms can be evaluated in binary machine code, we eliminate the higher level interpretations, thus providing an additional substantial speed enhancement. Evaluating strategies at this low level consumes the fewest CPU cycles, has the smallest power consumption footprint, the most efficient memory manipulation, requires no garbage collection, and the resultant linear structure may yield a more efficient search for some applications.[7] With so many possible machine level manipulations, operating at the register level offers the greatest potential to design fast, simple, unique and robust algorithms.

Machine level CPU throughput speed-up can be observed through the following example:

How many CPU cycles does it take to compute the following?

X = Y + Z

High level languages: 20 Clock cycles

CGPS(LAIMGP[8]): 1 Clock cycle

---

[6] http://msdn.microsoft.com/en-us/magazine/cc163717.aspx
[7] http://www.tradingsystemlab.com/files/CISC%20Architectures.pdf
[8] http://www.amazon.com/s?ie=UTF8&field-

Reference:

http://www.tradingsystemlab.com/files/CISC%20Architectures.pdf

So, immediately a speedup of 20 to 1 is realistic with the LAIMGP. Further speed up may be obtained through HT and many-core implementations. If we can develop and implement this overall algorithm approach within schedule, budget and technical limitations we might have an industry-leading machine designed approach.

One final important issue remains regarding the learning machine. What type of learning process should we employ? Should we use supervised learning, unsupervised learning or reinforcement learning? Should we attempt to predict some period into the future based on price or volatility? Or should we let the machine self-define its own trading structure without relying on prediction directly. To answer this let's look at several examples:

Which system would you trade?

System 1:

35% accurate and average Win is 180% of Average Loss.

System 2:

90% accurate and average Win is 10% of Average Loss.

To answer this question we must evaluate the expectation equation:

$EV = PW*AW - PL*AL$

Where

author=Frank%20D.%20Francone&page=1&rh=n%3A283155%2Cp_27%3AFrank%20D.%20Francone

EV = the expected value of the trading strategy

PW = the probability of a winning trade

PL = the probability of a losing trade

AW = the amount won in a winning trade

AL = the amount lost in a losing trade

Rearranging and noting that PL = 1 − PW we have:

EV = PW*(AW + AL) − AL

SIMULATION

With 3 unknowns this equation is unsolvable with an infinite number of solutions falling under the theoretically perfect equity curve where PW = 1.0 and AW = $1070 as is the case on the eMini S&P contract trading system as given in Figure 1 and Figure 2. To be very clear here, the theoretically perfect trading system equity curve is not possible in real time but is manufactured by looking ahead in time. What is noted is the shape of the curve, the total profit and the intraday peak to valley drawdown. We can target this theoretically perfect trading system equity curve's shape as well as overall net profit, drawdown, etc. through variations in the machine designed trading systems objective function.

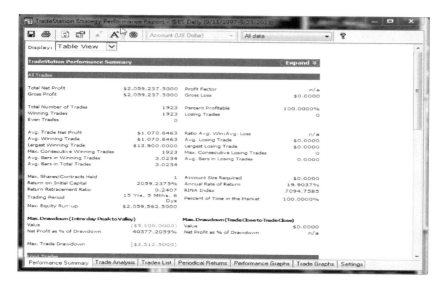

Figure 1. The theoretically perfect trading system

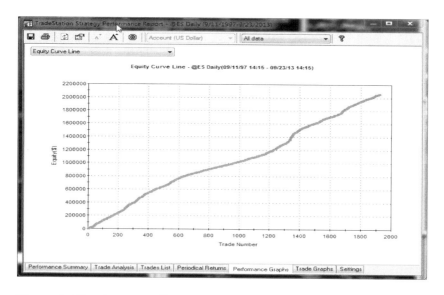

Figure 2. The theoretically perfect trading system equity curve (ES 1997-2013)

A typical trading system might capture only 15 % of the theoretically perfect trading system. An example of a typical trading system on the same market is shown in Figure 3.

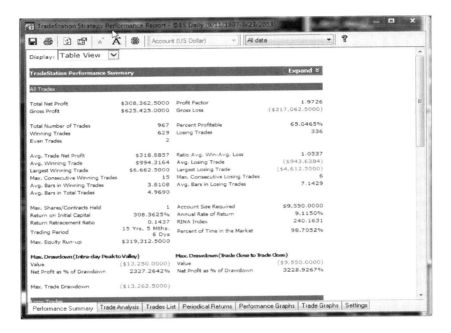

Figure 3. eMini S&P trading system

Returning to our question and plugging in the values into the EV equation we obtain the following expectations for System 1 and System 2:

System 1: EV = -.02

System 2: EV = -.01

So neither system should be traded. Note that a trading system that is 35% accurate may be very profitable yet a system that is 90% accurate may be unprofitable per the EV equation and simulations.

We still need to decide what variation of machine learning we should use. Should we base the approach on predictive analytics or other forms of machine learning[9][10]? If we are going to drill down deep into the data to extract alpha that has not been easily mined by other techniques and if we are going to avoid some of the biases that might be injected into the process we should consider not using predictive analytics. As we just showed, a system that is based only on accuracy of forecast can still lose money. What if we designed an open ended simulator that let the trading itself float, producing trades only when the learning algorithm indicates a trade? We can then see how the process performs over the entire data set and allow the learning algorithm to adjust the process as it trades. Thus the learning algorithm will learn to trade as it is trading within the simulator with no prediction process employed. So a development bias in deciding how far into the future to forecast does not need to me made! The trading strategy creates itself.

ENTRY TACTICS

Entry tactic is a critical component of any trading simulation. Some markets, due to their nature of trendiness, as evident by analysis of Indicator Serial Correlation,[11] prefer entering on a stop whereas other markets prefer to have entry tactics based on limit entries. It is believed that those markets that are countertrending in nature prefer entering on limit based entry tactics. There are many variations of entry tactics, some quite exotic. Additionally if the learning algorithm has the capabilities of exporting more than one output, the additional outputs can be used for the machine creation of multiple subsystems in one run. Typical entry tactics are shown

---

[9] http://en.wikipedia.org/wiki/Predictive_analytics
[10] http://en.wikipedia.org/wiki/Machine_learning
[11] http://www.tradingsystemlab.com/

in Table 2.

```
1.  This Bar's Close
2.  This Bar's Close +/- Stop
3.  Next Bar's Open
4.  NextOpen+/- Stop
5.  Enter on Limit
6.  Next Bar on Stop
7.  Enter on Limit non Stop/Rev
8.  Ent on Close or Next Open+/- Stop
9.  Ent on Stop or Close
10. Ent on Close or Next Open
11. Ent on Close, Next Open or Stop
12. Ent on a GPStop: use 62n data
13. Ent on Close +/- Limit
14. Next Bar's Open +/- Limit
15. Next Bar's Close (Mutual Funds)
16. Ent/Ex Nxt Bar GP Stop non Stop/Rev
17. NxtOpn+/-Limit or Close+/-Limit
18. Next Bar's Open +/- Stop Mod1
19. Enter on Stop or Limit
```

Table 2. Entry Tactics

OBJECTIVE FUNCTIONS

We have covered the learning process and the trading simulator but what goal should we target since we are not targeting a predicted or dependent variable? Since the strategy self-creates, we can target any normally used trading system metric or create a new objective function, or goal. Table 3 shows some commonly used metrics for trading strategies. Once the fitness routines are in place it becomes easy to implement any fitness objective function other than the ones below.

1. Net Profit
2. Net Profit/StdDev Return
3. Net Profit/(StdDev Return ^2)
4. Net Profit/Max Drawdown
5. Sharpe Ratio
6. Average Trade/Max Drawdown
7. (Average Trade * Net Profit)/StdDev Return
8. (Average Trade * Net Profit)/(StdDev Return^2)
9. Net Profit/SQRT(StdDev Return)
10. Net Profit/(FlatTime^2)
11. Average Return/StdDev Return
12. Net Profit/FlatTime
13. Average Return*Average Trade
14. Average Return/SQRT(Max drawdown)
15. Net Profit/SQRT(Max Drawdown)
16. Average Trade
17. Profit Factor
18. Percent Accuracy
19. Profit Factor*Percent Accuracy*Net Profit
20. Profit Factor*Net Profit
21. Net Profit/Largest Losing Trade
22. Net Profit/Average Losing Trade
23. Average Maximum Retracement
24. Log(Net Profit)/Max Drawdown
25. Average Return/Max Drawdown
26. Profit Factor*Percent Accuracy/Max Drawdown
27. Net Profit/SQRT(Semivariance)
28. Recent Return Weighted
29. Pessimistic Return Ratio (Vince)
30. Sharpe Ratio + TotTrades
31. Net Profit/Max Drawdown + TotTrades
32. Net Profit/Semivariance
33. PF+TotTrades
34. Net Profit*CorrToPerfectEquityCurve
35. Net Profit*(CorrToPerfectEquityCurve^2)
36. NetProfit/TimeInMarket
37. AverageTrade/SQRT(MaxDrawdown)
38. NetProfit*AvgTrade
39. NetProfit*(AvgTrade^2)
40. SQRT(TotTrades)*AverageTrade

Table 3. Objective Functions

If we are using a "design itself" paradigm for our machine designed trading system algorithm we notice that objective functions become blurred and cross impacting. For example, say you are targeting only Net Profit as an objective function. The inverse of Net Profit is an error function that is desired to be minimized. We notice the effect in Figure 4. In this example, although we target 1/Net Profit as the Error Function, as this error is minimized, drawdown also decreases even though we did not specifically target drawdown within the objective function. Additional trading system metrics firm up as well while we choose only 1/Net Profit as the objective function.

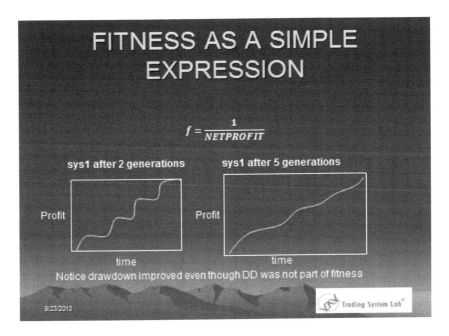

Figure 4. Objective Function Cross Impact

TRANSLATIONS

At this point we have addressed the learning machine, trading simulator and objective function however we have yet to address the implementation issue of language translation. Machine code is very low level code so unless we wish to conduct development operations only at this low level we must have translations to higher level languages. Machine code will need to be up-translated to a typical algorithmic trading language like C or C# and then if required, again translated to a trading platform language such as Easy Language® or Power Language.

CONCLUSION

In conclusion, we have outlined the process to develop an algorithm that designs another algorithm, in this case a trading algorithm. We have reviewed the learning algorithm, the simulation algorithm, the objective functions and the translation routines. We have argued that difficult and costly approaches might offer the best chance of finding robust alpha in the financial time series data we mine. We have shown that the theoretically perfect trading system may be used as a target for our machine learning process and that allowing the algorithm to design itself with minimal constraints from the developer might offer the greatest chance for success.

For more information contact Michael L. Barna at:
mike@tradingsystemlab.com
www.tradingsystemlab.com

How to Increase Your Trading Profits with the New THD Directional Volume Indicator by Gail Mercer

When I first started studying volume, I lost more money than I made. Figuring out where to analyze the volume bars and even deciding if I needed to use a moving average of the volume were questions that I just couldn't seem to answer. Was every volume bar significant? Or did I need to only analyze the volume bars that exceeded the moving average? If so, what was the magical number of volume bars to use in the moving average? It seemed that each new question, lead to other questions. So I went back to the founding father of volume analysis, Richard Wyckoff to find answers.

Wyckoff analyzed volume as price made new highs, new lows or tested a previous high or low. Since I love reading price bars and I am an expert at reading highs and lows, I knew this was where I needed to start. Since changes in volume precede price movement, I did not want to use a moving average. Moving averages are designed to smooth price and identify trend. The smoothing typically creates a lag. It made no sense to me to turn a leading indicator into a lagging indicator. Instead, it would be more beneficial, in my opinion, to learn to read volume at critical areas and maintain the non-lagging benefit of volume analysis.

What is confusing to many new traders, is that volume indicators are typically non-directional. This means that as new highs are formed, new highs in volume should form. However, when new lows are formed, new highs in volume should form. This makes the volume indicator non-directional. This can be confusing when trying to learn volume because traders expect volume to move with price. There is a common misconception that "price is moving down and, therefore, volume should move down." The exact opposite is the case, however. This misconception is one of the reasons that I was drawn to Cumulative Delta Volume Analysis – unlike other volume indicators, Cumulative Delta moves *with* price and appears on the charts just like price bars. The only drawback is that it is an uncommon charting type and not all charting packages offer it. Thankfully, Multicharts now offer Cumulative Delta as a charting type and, if a trader has an account with Ampfutures, then the cumulative delta data is free via CQG.

Since I knew the issues that make it difficult for traders to effectively use volume, I could design an indicator that would overcome these issues. This lead to the development of the TradersHelpDesk (THD) Directional Volume indicator for intraday charts. First, I plotted the color of the volume bar according to whether the price bar made a high, low, inside bar, or outside bar. These four components are critical to knowing *where* to analyze the volume. For example, you must wait for either an inside bar or a close down, after a high, before reading volume. Using a color code for defining the price bar types now makes reading volume easier because the color is derived from the price bar action.

Now, I needed a way to show who controlled the actual bar, buyers or sellers. First, I plotted a zero line. If the volume is above zero, buyers are controlling the bar. If the volume is below zero, sellers are controlling the bar. The result is a volume indicator, that is directional (meaning it is easier for traders to understand) and enables traders to read volume on the live edge of the market at a glance.

Although I use other colors on my intraday charts, for clarity purposes, the THD Directional Volume indicator color codes on the following images are:

New High (when compared to previous bar)=Dark Blue

New Low (when compared to previous bar)=Red

Inside Bar (when compared to previous bar)=Dark Gray

Outside Bar (when compared to previous bar)=Magenta

In **Figure 1: Crude Oil Three Minute Chart**, the THD Directional Volume indicator is on the bottom of the chart and the price bars are colored using the THD Trend indicator. The plus sign (+) indicates where the ATR stop is located (which is built into the THD Trend indicator). At Point A, notice that the first red bar is below zero, which indicates that price made a low and sellers controlled the bar. On the second red bar, sellers made a low but BUYERS controlled the bar (volume divergence). This occurred right at the ATR stop, which is the lowest point of risk and a long position could be entered at the close of this bar (101.51). Price then began moving up (Point B). Price reached a high of 101.79 and sellers stepped in because the volume bar plotted below zero (sellers controlled the bar). The close of the bar was 101.69 and since the price bar was a down bar, the divergence can be read at that moment, generating an exit.

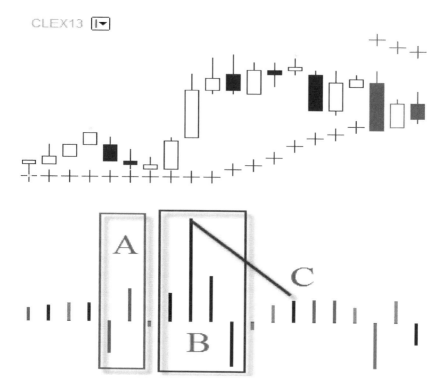

Figure 1: Crude Oil Three Minute Chart

The THD ATR Stop on the trade was at 101.48 and I tell my students to offset the ATR by two or three ticks. In this case, a hard stop at 101.45 (three ticks) would be adequate. The total risk on the trade would be six ticks and the total reward was eighteen ticks. This gave a risk to reward ratio of 1:3 (one tick of risk for three ticks of reward).

Another option on this trade would be to take a portion of the trade off at twelve ticks (a one to two risk to reward ratio on the first portion of the position) and then move the stop to breakeven plus the cost of the trade (101.53). You could then set additional profit targets or you could exit the remainder of the position if additional divergence occur at Point C (101.76) or when the ATR stop was flipped (which occurred at 101.60).

The THD Directional Volume indicator can also be used to exit a trade early. For example, in *Figure 2: Gold Three Minute Chart*, at Point A an identical entry to the short side was indicated. Price had pulled back to the ATR stop, on decreasing buying volume. A short position of the close of the bar was generated (1329.7). The ATR Stop was at 1330.1. Offsetting the ATR stop by two ticks, a hard stop was placed at 1330.3 resulting in a risk of six ticks.

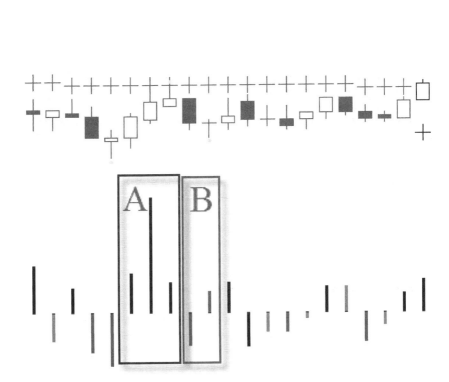

Figure 2: Gold Three Minute Chart

Then at Point B, on the first down bar, sellers stepped back in as expected. However, on the next bar down bar, although a low was made, the buyers controlled the bar (volume bar plotted above zero). This indicated volume divergence on the selling side and an exit was generated at the close of the bar or 1329. The reward on this trade was only seven ticks and the risk to reward was only slightly greater than one to one (risking six ticks and only making seven ticks). Although this is not the ideal risk to reward, the early exit was identified by an unanticipated volume divergence on the seller's side.

Alternatively, instead of exiting the trade, the hard stop could be modified to breakeven plus the cost of the trade or 1329.50. In this scenario, either price moved in the anticipated direction or the trade was exited with no loss.

Both of these examples (Figures 1 and 2) are using only one timeframe. However, the power of volume analysis can be seen when applying this same technique to higher timeframes (higher profits). In other words, instead of focusing only on a three minute chart, a higher timeframe may used to identify the ideal entry or exit.

In **Figure 3: AUDUSD 60 Minute Chart**, using the same setup (pullback to the ATR stop on diverging volume), price had pulled back to the ATR stop on diverging buying volume. A short entry was generated and, since this is a sixty minute chart, instead of offsetting the ATR by two or three ticks, the offset would be at least ten ticks. Entry was indicated at the close of the bar that generated the divergence (second blue volume bar labeled Point A) or .9360 and a hard stop was set at .9380 (twenty ticks of risk per contract). At the Point B, when the gray volume bar formed, an exit would be generated at .9309. This is the point where the volume divergence can be read because gray indicates an inside bar. The trade netted fifty-one ticks of profits per contract, while only risking twenty ticks per contract.

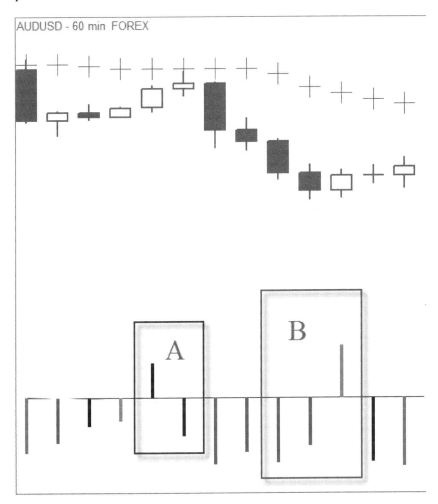

Figure 3: AUDUSD 60 Minute Chart

The truth is volume does lead price. However, as Richard Wyckoff often said, volume alone is not the solution. It is the overall market conditions and the ability to create a decisive methodology that incorporates a low risk entry which is then followed day in and day out that makes a trader successful. This is what sets my training and indicators apart from others.

First, I teach traders how to read both price and volume bars. Second, I have created a suite of indicators that identify which markets to trade, when to expect retracements and how to identify the area where price will retrace. Next, I will help you create your own unique trading plan that incorporates price, volume and trend identification with a low risk entry setup. My job does not stop there. I know firsthand how lonely and isolated trading can be. Having someone to call or ask a question is critically important when trying to understand the markets and read the price bars. That's why my clients know they can call or e-mail me directly when they are confused or struggling.

That's the TradersHelpDesk difference! For more information on the TradersHelpDesk indicators, methodology, or training sessions, visit my website at www.TradersHelpDesk.com. Of course, if you have any questions, please email me at gm@tradershelpdesk.com.

Ninjacators Real Time Supply and Demand Indicator Intro to the Indicator Of The Month Club By Troy Epperson

The Real time Supply and Demand Indicator is one of Ninjacators FREE indicators from the Ninjacators' indicator of the month club. Ninjacators' indicators are made to be used on the NINJA TRADER trading platform only. NINJA TRADER is available for free and there is a link on our website www.ninjacators.com that will direct you to that download.

Why should you join over 12,000 traders who get a FREE indicator and trading strategy from us every month? Because, you'll love playing with the innovative indicators we come up with to help you make more profitable trades with NinjaTrader — all of which have been field tested with real money trades. You'll have a no-hassle, no-risk way to try out new indicators and trading methods without having to spend a dime. The indicator of the month club is your first step to having the kind of success you've always wanted with your trades. Each month you'll get a free indicator, and our famous one sheet PDF explaining the trading strategy behind it. Plus, you'll get an invitation to a live Q&A webcast showing you how to use the indicator in a wide range of trading scenarios.

All absolutely free.

You'll also occasionally get exclusive offers, with aggressive member only discounts, on indicator bundles and video training to help make an immediate difference in your trading success. The bottom line is — we don't want you to just take our word for how effective our indicators and trading strategies are. We want you to put them through their paces like the other 12,000+ traders in the club have, and see for yourself if our indicators – and real world trading strategies — really click for you. To give it a try just fill in the form below at www.Ninjacators.com, and your first indicator and trading strategy will be sent to you immediately. We'll never share your email with anyone else and you can decrease, increase or stop getting emails from us at any time.

Just give us your first name and email address and click the join now to start receiving the free indicator of the month!

Ninjacators Real Time Supply and Demand Indicator

The Real time Supply and Demand indicator captures the core function of every market – Supply and Demand. Supply and Demand is the reason why the markets move!

When Supply is bigger than Demand – the price will fall ... When Demand is bigger than Supply – the price will rise. It is really that simple.

When Supply and Demand are the same or "in balance" the price will not move either way. The Real time Supply and Demand indicator identifies areas where Supply and Demand is out of balance and when these areas apply there are great trading opportunities. The indicator plots the "zones" in real time on your chart.

All calculation are made in Real-time, the indicator does not calculate or plot historical zones. Every zone which gets "run over" by the price will disappear from the chart and will not repaint. As we track real time buying and selling zones new zones will be plotted as soon as the indicator detects an imbalance of buyers and sellers and other zones will disappear as they are not of further interest because the buying and selling will take place at a different area. There are two types of alerts to assist you with entries. Visual alerts are triggered when retest/re-entry occurs and the zone with change color from Red to Coral or from Green to Light Green depending on whether it is a Supply or Demand Zone. At the same time you will also get an auditory alert (this can be customized to your own .wav file).

Best Trading Strategies

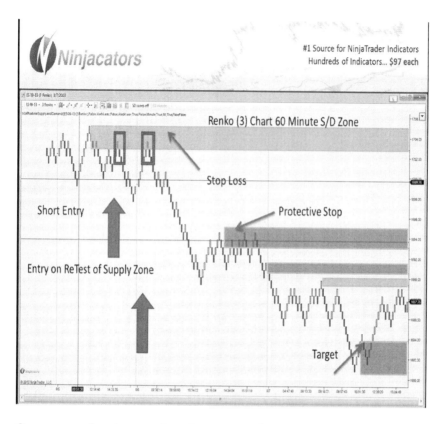

Once a zone has been painted, you wait for a retest of that zone and fade the zone. On the picture above once the coral zone paints when price moves up to re-test or re-enter the zone you enter a short position using the top of the supply zone as your stop loss. As new supply zones are formed they provide areas to move protective stops to. These protective stops allow you to stay in the trade longer only exiting the trade if the supply zone is breached. At the bottom of the chart a Demand zone is formed and when price exits this zone (buyers provided demand and price went up) it is time to exit the short position since the Demand Zone was not breached to the downside. We have found that the first instance of retest or re-entry is the highest probability entry although secondary retests are good entry's as well. When zones are created during off-market hours please use caution when trading those zones as the lack of data during those times can compromise the statistical relevance of the zones.

The indicator can be used in any market and on any timeframe. It is also customizable to handle non-time charts like Renko, Range or Volume charts. An additional feature is that the indicator does not have to use the chart as the basis for its calculation allowing you to have "Zones" that are plotted on the chart that are not dependent on type of chart. For Example you may have a 5 minute chart with Supply and Demand Zones based on a 60 minute calculation. Of course this indicator is highly customizable so entry prices of the zones may be displayed on the chart and zones can be extended past real time into the future. Multiple "time" zones may be displayed and colors can be modified to help differentiate between time zones. This system can be used as a stand-alone or as a complementary part of an existing system.

This indicator has over 6000 lines of code and therefore is very data sensitive, so traders need to manage their data appropriately. For intra-day charting we recommend using 5 days of data or less. When initially loading indicator use small amounts of data since it is a real time indicator a large amount of data is NOT needed. Please keep in mind that the indicator is a real time indicator with no historical plot. Back testing is best done with the Market Replay.

Summary:

Real Time Supply and Demand Indicator

Any market

Any timeframe

Any type of chart

Multi-time frame calculations

Showing you the very core of every market (supply and demand)

Call to Action!

Join Free Indicator of the Month Club

http://www.ninjacators.com/indicator-of-the-month-club/

Download NinjaTrader

Download Ninjacators Indicator of the Month

Start using Ninjacators' Indicators to enhance your trading!

APA Zones Exposing the Hidden Order Flow by Gabriel Brent

Hello everyone, and thank you for taking time out of your busy schedule to see an amazing perspective on the markets that not many know about. As always, please realize that trading and investing has risks and not all individuals should trade or invest. At APA Zones, we are looking at why the markets move the way they do. If we can understand the "why", then statistically, knowing what's going to happen next is not so hard because we have now have context and a frame of reference.

We really need to start at the beginning to begin to understand the "why". So, where is the beginning? Is it the beginning of your chart; the beginning of time; the beginning of the US session? Those are all good beginnings but we are looking to find out what drives the market. Anyone know what two ideas drive practically all markets? It all goes back to Adam Smith and supply and demand. It's the order flow of supply and demand - buyers and sellers that really push the markets.

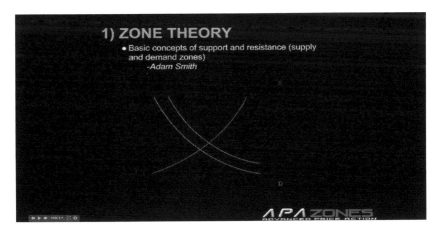

Best Trading Strategies

(Basic supply and demand moves the market. We can then look at other factors, like the news, that either speed up these moves exponentially, or reverse price at key areas.)

Shifting supply and demand curves that change over time is affecting the market that you are watching right now.

This is happening not only on the macro level of big daily bars but also on the micro level of 1 minute charts and 1 range bars.

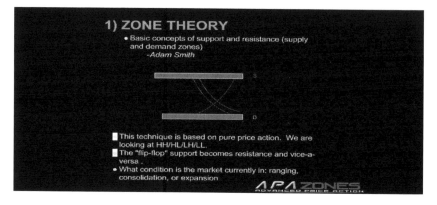

(See how supply is above demand on the right side of the graph)

Now, as we apply these simple concepts of supply and demand, we see that an excess of supply exists on the top of this graph and an excess of demand exists on the bottom of the graph.

However, in order to understand how complex these simple principles can get, we need the aid of a computer to help us keep track of all the supply and demand levels and what they look like on their many different timeframes. We see so much trading activity aided by computer algorithms, dark pools, high frequency traders, and the like that we are beginning to see special reports about all these exploits of the capital markets. It's time that we start using our multi-core, beasts of PCs to calculate more than what the average price was for the last 20 bars. We need to record what these systems are seeing and what these systems are responding to. What is really important to the market movement is support and resistance and supply and demand - something that only a few systematic traders can see and comprehend on a multiple day, weekly or monthly basis, or in a multiple timeframe analysis.

The majority of us are just trying to figure out what setting of MACD we should use day to day. What we actually need is for our beefy computers to work for us and tell us when we are in an area of wholesale or retail (supply or demand).

Now, the concepts that we are going to be covering from here on out are not for the novice trader. We are going to be making some extremely complex mathematical equations look really simple, but that's what we love to do: make complex systems easy to use. If you had a system that could tell you when price is at proven and dynamic supply or demand levels based on market price action, what would that be worth to you? You would no longer have to guess at why the market is moving the way it is. You would be able to see where the supply level, or zone, as we like to call it, is at. And, you would be able to see price moving away from the zone. Now, something that almost every trader out there will tell you is, "trade with the trend". But what IS "the trend"? Well, if you are like us, then the trend is very subjective since we look at different approaches and systems. It is at this point that we can use the typical charts that other investors, swing traders, and daytraders use to give us an edge that most traders do not have.

Best Trading Strategies

(Here is a basic chart. Why are bars where they are? What do these bars tell us is going to happen next?)

Here is a basic chart which shows price moving up and down. What is the time frame? What market is it on? With the way we look at charts, these things don't really matter because there is a lot more going on here than meets the eye. Price and order flow tell us the whole story but we have to be in tune with that story so that we can keep track of how and why the story is unfolding. Who likes to start reading a book in the middle? No one, of course. If you haven't read from the beginning, then there is no context for why things are happening or who the characters are. We need to take the same approach to reading the markets. Maybe this book shares similarities with another book that you read last year, or maybe not. If you don't have the context in which to put things when reading price action, then you will never know the whole story. The same is true in the markets. If we have no context for why the market is doing what it's doing, then we are not going to be able to make good trading decisions. Maybe this price action is exactly the same as last year's, or maybe not. However, when we consistently apply the ideas of supply and demand to the zones, we get an all together clearer picture because we gain context.

(Zones with green numbers on the right are demand zones, and zones with red numbers are supply zones.)

Since the computer is now working for us to plot levels of supply and demand and monitor them for us, we have context for order flow. With market memory of dynamic levels, we now have context. There are a lot of different color zones on this chart. These color zones help us know which side is weaker and when supply and demand are, more than likely, going to shift. The software keeps track of the order flow that will, in the future, make that level important or not. The colors help us see how many times a particular zone has been re-tested by price action. This re-testing helps us identify the shifts in supply and demand just like we see on the supply and demand curve charts that play out in our markets. Now, as we look at the range that this market has had, we can see some very interesting things. First, we are looking at a weekly chart, so while many traders may be seeing the trend over a number of days, we are seeing range, knowing where the tops and bottoms of the range are going to be. Second, we see a new demand zone forming in between the range which means buyers, or demand, has shifted so can expect to see price go higher and break above the current range.

Now, let's put all that we have discussed into a real world example. I'm sure many of you have been watching the markets for at least a little while now, and have noticed that as financial news comes out, the market reacts to it in crazy ways. Sometimes the reaction is the exact opposite of what you would think it would be. How can poor employment numbers surface and result in the market rocketing up? How interesting that the market would think that having more people out of work would be good, when it seems so wrong. Unfortunately, the market is not in touch with its emotional side and does not think in the same ways that we do. We are going to burst your bubble, now, and tell you what the hidden order flow may have been telling us all along. We need to think about why the market is doing what it's doing. What are the masses thinking? What are large institutions doing? News flash: They want to make money! Do they care where your orders are? Not really, but they need someone to take the other side of their trade. Your account will work just as well as that of a dark pool account or an HFT(high frequency trader). What we need to realize is that all of these different institutions have to program out something or systematic trade something that is repeatable and that is dynamic over time. It must be able to self adjust no matter what the time of day or year. If you watch the news and price seems to move in a direction that is not only non-sensecal, but also seems wrong, it is because price is actually following laws that are beyond your field of vision. It is just finishing its move from supply and demand and it needs a catalyst to do it.

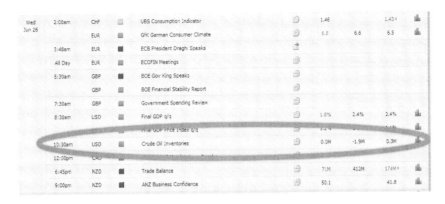

(The crude oil inventories news announcement was better than expected or forecasted.)

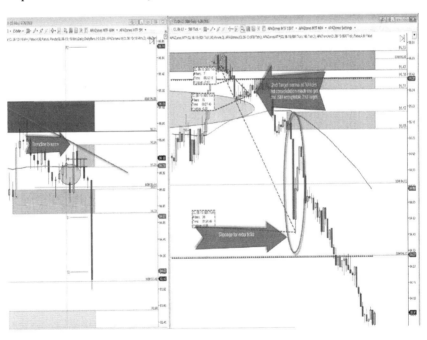

(The crude oil market was in a downward move between supply and demand accelerating the move that we would expect, but going against positive news.)

As in the example of the crude oil inventories setup that we posted above, we can see that the real move was one from a supply area, as well as a trend line bounce off of a much higher time frame. Then the craziness of the inventories news announcement comes out. This news causes an exponential expansion of price movement from supply down to demand. This is highlighted on the charts with the two 60 minute (60M) zones, red rays, and price moving from the 60M zone to the green zone (or green rays).

The reasons the market moves is not complicated but it does take some work and study so that you can understand the dynamic shifts and movements between supply and demand and hidden order flow areas. Supply and demand is a perfect system for larger institutions and more educated traders to create an edge in their trading by simply following its laws.

How to Predict the Closing Direction of Any Market by Scott Andrews

There may be no more stressful and frustrating experience than to see a large opening gap and not know what to do. Will the markets close up or down today? Should I take profits? Cut my losses? Get short? Add to my position? Like a deer in headlights, you freeze and wait - *hoping* for the best outcome.

But often the market move is substantial, erasing a large portion of your profits or forcing you to 'chase' or hope for a pullback. And *this* is the difference between the Wall Street 'Pros' and the Main Street 'Joes.

The Pros take action *before* the market moves against them. Like sheep led to the slaughter, the Joes wait and pray - often costing them hundreds or thousands of dollars in potential profits. The accuracy by which a trader can predict today's closing price will ultimately determine the size of his profits (or losses).

How do the Pros know? They don't. But they do know the historically-based probabilities for any given day and market scenario. The Joes however often take their cues from the myriad of pundits on financial news stations or online (where any Joe can pose as a Pro) or via their ability to "read" the charts.

So how can today's retail trader gain the same data-driven advantages as Wall Street? The answer lies in weather forecasting.

At the end of World War I, many meteorologists had begun to believe that scientifically accurate weather prediction was more a fantasy than a potential reality. But then a an English mathematician named Lewis Richardson began using physics to emulate the factors creating the weather over Europe. The basis of his approach has been further leveraged by the advent of super-computers.

Today, modern weather forecasting is based on using an "ensemble" of many differing models to create the most likely future weather scenarios. The key concept is that the more different models suggesting the same outcome, the more likely it is to occur.

The basic premise of ensemble forecasting can be applied to financial forecasting and this approach has served me well over the past 10 years of active investing and trading. Fortunately, the same level of sophistication and granularity of national weather forecasting is not needed in order to benefit from its power as a trader and investor. Simply evaluating a given setup by three or more unrelated or lowly-correlated analytical methods can greatly increase the accuracy and usefulness of back-testing.

To anticipate the most likely closing direction of a market (i.e. stock, future or commodity) for a given day, I evaluate the size and direction of the opening gap in the context of current Momentum, Volatility, Overbought/Oversold, Trend, and Seasonality pressures. My Bayesian / Ensemble approach is based on research I've created over the years while trading the opening gap, as well as innovative, industry-leading technical approaches developed by other industry technicians such as John Bollinger and Welles Wilder.

Gap size is based on fixed percentages of the five(5) day Average True Range (ATR). The True Range is the greater of the difference between the high and low of a session, or the difference between the prior close and the high or low of a session. By considering the prior close, the size of any unfilled opening gaps is included in the analysis of the daily range making it representative of the "true" market movement for that day.

"PF" is an abbreviation for Profit Factor - a term which represents the ratio of historical, simulated profits and losses. If PF is > 1 then that scenario has made more money than it lost during the back-tested period, the bigger the better of course. For example, a PF of 2 means that twice as many profits were generated than losses. If the PF is < 1, then the scenario has lost money historically, i.e. its profits were smaller than its total losses.

Since 2003, 54% (1,206 / 2,242) of opening gaps of at least 1 point in size (ES, or ~10 cents in the SPY) have closed HIGHER than their open by the end of the day. Though showing a slight bullish bias, this bias can be amplified or reversed when considering the gap size and direction. **Exhibit 1** shows the significant edge gap size and direction provide into the odds of the S&P 500 closing higher on a given day.

Closing Odds by Opening Gap Direction & Size with EOD Exit (S&P 500)

Gap Direction & Size (% of 5 day ATR)	# Trades	% Close Higher	Hypothetical Profit Factor	Hypothetical Net Profit
Large Up Gap (>80%)	64	62%	1.45	$ 46,375
Medium Up Gap (>40%)	301	55%	1.41	$ 226,750
Small Up Gap (<40%)	833	53%	0.97	$ 46,375
Small Down Gap (<40%)	692	56%	1.05	$ 61,750
Medium Down Gap (>40%)	277	51%	0.86	$ (102,250)
Large Down Gap (>80%)	75	47%	0.74	$ (62,625)

Copyright ClosingOdds.com - All rights reserved

Test parameters: Hypothetical trades, 10 years (2004-2013), ES, excludes nominal gaps, exit at 4:00 pm ET, commissions & slippage not included

Best Trading Strategies

Exhibit 1: Closing Odds by Opening Gap Direction and Size

"Momentum" is the measure of acceleration of a security's price in a specific direction. The concept is that the stronger the momentum, the greater the likelihood of continuing in that direction. Welles Wilder created two helpful indicators that can be used in conjunction with one another to measure momentum: RSI and ADX.

RSI stands for Relative Strength Index. Contrary to its name, it does not measure the relative strength of individual stocks or indices to one another. Instead RSI measures the average closing gain of a security to the average closing loss of its prior "X" sessions. Strong momentum to the upside is found with readings of 70-80 or higher, and to the downside with readings of 20-30 or lower.

ADX is also known as the Average Directional Index and it measures the strength of a prevailing trend by comparing two other indicators by Wilder: a positive directional indicator (+DI) and a negative directional indicator (-DI). ADX combines and soothes the two into an exponential moving average. Though it does not provide an indication of direction, it is an excellent way to confirm the strength of a trend. Depending on the market, a reading less than 20-25 generally indicates a non-trending environment.

By combining RSI and ADX, a market's directional momentum can be determined and used for assessing the odds of closing higher or lower.

Exhibit 2 shows the 10 year results of going long the S&P 500 e-mini futures for all small down gaps at the open (9:30 am ET) and exiting at the end of the day (4:00 pm ET) based upon 12 different momentum classifications.

\multicolumn{5}{c}{Closing Odds by Momentum (for small down gaps)}
Condition #	# Trades	% Close Higher	Hypothetical Profit Factor	Hypothetical Net Profit
1	97	54	0.98	$ (1,750.00)
2	93	62	1.42	$ 36,125.00
3	45	53	1.37	$ 33,875.00
4	54	69	1.59	$ 44,625.00
5	93	62	1.48	$ 64,875.00
6	73	59	1.22	$ 23,625.00
7	53	51	0.75	$ (45,875.00)
8	56	41	0.61	$ (72,875.00)
9	45	56	0.93	$ (6,500.00)
10	36	50	0.79	$ (15,500.00)
11	20	30	0.28	$ (51,875.00)
12	27	70	1.97	$ 53,000.00

Test parameters: Hypothetical trades, 10 years (2004-2013), ES, excludes nominal gaps, exit at 4:00 pm ET, commissions & slippage not included

Exhibit 2: Closing Odds by Momentum (for small down gaps)

Note: In order to highlight the value of the various market conditions and eliminate the significant impact of gap size and direction, Exhibit 2 and the remaining tables only show the results for "small down gaps" (<40% of the 5 day ATR).

"Volatility" can be measured in terms of range contraction and expansion. When gauged across different time frames, it is very effective for identifying when a security is poised and overdue for a significant move in either direction. Vice versa, after periods of extreme movement a security will often consolidate.

Exhibit 3 shows the 10 year historical results of going long the S&P 500 e-mini futures for all small down gaps at the open (9:30 am ET)

and exiting at the end of the day (4:00 pm ET) based upon 12 different volatility classifications.

Closing Odds by Volatility (for small down gaps)

Condition #	# Trades	% Close Higher	Hypothetical Profit Factor	Hypothetical Net Profit
1	99	54	0.97	$ (4,250.00)
2	71	58	1.45	$ 45,250.00
3	87	59	1.46	$ 50,000.00
4	97	63	1.33	$ 45,625.00
5	51	55	0.98	$ (1,250.00)
6	62	58	1.06	$ 4,750.00
7	26	46	0.73	$ (20,750.00)
8	16	56	0.97	$ (1,750.00)
9	45	51	0.84	$ (18,625.00)
10	49	65	1.85	$ 69,000.00
11	44	48	0.55	$ (71,000.00)
12	45	51	0.72	$ (35,250.00)

Test parameters: Hypothetical trades, 10 years (2004-2013), ES, excludes nominal gaps, exit at 4:00 pm ET, commissions & slippage not included

Exhibit 3: Closing Odds by Volatility (for small down gaps)

"Overbought and Oversold" (OB/OS) conditions describe when an asset's price has moved too far, too fast and may be over or under valued and due for a pause or pullback. Though this technical term is somewhat subjective it can be quantified statistically and is very helpful for determining the odds of a security closing higher on a given day.

Perhaps the best known and widely used OB/OS measure was created by John Bollinger and uses standard deviations to create statistical bands of potential support and resistance.

Exhibit 4 shows the 10 year historical results of going long the S&P 500 e-mini futures for all small down gaps at the open (9:30 am ET) and exiting at the end of the day (4:00 pm ET) based upon 10 different Overbought/Oversold classifications.

Closing Odds by Overbought/Oversold (for small down gaps)

Condition #	# Trades	% Close Higher	Hypothetical Profit Factor	Hypothetical Net Profit
1	47	62	1.63	$ 23,250.00
2	124	60	1.50	$ 61,750.00
3	137	53	0.94	$ (11,875.00)
4	106	60	1.15	$ 26,125.00
5	48	63	1.62	$ 53,625.00
6	60	55	1.09	$ 12,375.00
7	55	53	1.08	$ 9,500.00
8	57	49	0.56	$ (98,875.00)
9	35	57	1.11	$ 6,875.00
10	23	39	0.76	$ (21,000.00)

Test parameters: Hypothetical trades, 10 years (2004-2013), ES, excludes nominal gaps, exit at 4:00 pm ET, commissions & slippage not included

Exhibit 4: Closing Odds by Overbought/Oversold conditions (for small down gaps)

"Trend" can be defined as the general direction of a market or security over a period of time. When a well-defined trend can be identified, it often pays to trade in that direction as closing odds will favor the trend. There are many ways to measure a trend, but there may be no more useful approach than to simply use the location of an asset's price relative to the high and lows of its prior "X" periods.

Exhibit 5 shows the 10 year historical results of going long the S&P 500 e-mini futures for all small down gaps at the open (9:30 am ET) and exiting at the end of the day (4:00 pm ET) based upon 7 different trend conditions.

Closing Odds by Trend (for small down gaps)

Condition #	# Trades	% Close Higher	Hypothetical Profit Factor	Hypothetical Net Profit
1	162	61	1.72	$ 93,875.00
2	93	61	1.26	$ 33,375.00
3	79	53	0.77	$ (36,375.00)
4	108	60	1.14	$ 23,875.00
5	81	47	0.87	$ (22,375.00)
6	105	53	0.99	$ (2,500.00)
7	64	52	0.89	$ (28,125.00)

Test parameters: Hypothetical trades, 10 years (2004-2013), ES, excludes nominal gaps, exit at 4:00 pm ET, commissions & slippage not included

Exhibit 5: Closing Odds by Trend (for small down gaps)

"Seasonality" means different things to different traders but for the purposes of closing odds analysis it refers primarily to the day of week (e.g. Monday, Tuesday, etc.). Though simple to calculate, it may be the most underrated and underappreciated of all technical approaches.

Exhibit 6 shows the 10 year historical results of going long the S&P 500 e-mini futures for all small down gaps at the open (9:30 am ET)

and exiting at the end of the day (4:00 pm ET) based upon 10 different Seasonality conditions.

Closing Odds by Seasonality (for small down gaps)

Condition #	# Trades	% Close Higher	Hypothetical Profit Factor	Hypothetical Net Profit
1	87	56	0.89	$ (12,250.00)
2	93	55	0.92	$ (12,625.00)
3	103	64	1.25	$ 43,875.00
4	87	59	1.24	$ 29,125.00
5	73	51	1.08	$ 12,000.00
6	45	51	0.77	$ (18,875.00)
7	50	48	1.00	$ -
8	58	55	1.04	$ 5,625.00
9	46	76	1.88	$ 75,375.00
10	50	44	0.56	$ (60,500.00)

Test parameters: Hypothetical trades, 10 years (2004-2013), ES, excludes nominal gaps, exit at 4:00 pm ET, commissions & slippage not included

Exhibit 6: Closing Odds by Seasonality (for small down gaps)

Whether you want to day trade the action or optimize your swing trade entries and exits, knowing the closing odds can help you make the best decisions for your account. If you would like to learn more and have daily probabilities for a number of futures and ETFs markets delivered to your inbox for free, simply sign up at ClosingOdds.com. Give it a try and let history be your guide!

For more information go to www.closingodds.com

UNCOMPLICATE YOUR TRADING BY AL MCWHIRR

I would like to thank TradersWorld for the opportunity to participate in their TradersWorld 14 online expo. I also would like to encourage all traders to consider using NinjaTrader for their charting. The software and support is superior.

In my previous writings, specifically my contribution in the **Finding Your Trading Method** Kindle book, as well as my article in **TradersWorld Magazine,** issue #55, I talk about auto trading. In this writing, I will be focused on manual trading.

Although many traders would love to be able to have a software program do their trading for them, in reality this is probably not going to happen. In my opinion, the majority of traders use a variety of indicators for their trading and as such, most auto trade methods and systems use indicators as well. Logically, if the indicators don't seem to work for those trading manually, chances are they will not be successful for auto trading. There are just too many variables that must be considered with auto trade methods that use indicators for signal entry. Although our EminiScalp Pilot Auto Trade does **not** use indicators for trade entries, a trader still must be aware of some of the intricacies of the market(s) they wish to trade. Whether trading manually or with an auto trade, there is a learning curve, as there is no way around this.

I have had traders ask me why they would have to learn anything if the auto trade does the trading for them. I respond by stating that there are a multitude of markets as well as a wide variety of time frames within these markets. It is imperative that a trader be aware of when their particular market opens and closes as well as when there may be any news that may impact their chosen market. They should also be aware of the way the market moves within the trading day. Does the particular market slow down at lunch? Does the range get narrow during this time? How is trading in the pre-market? What generally happens as the market draws to a close? What happens immediately before and after news? These are points that need to be considered. No auto trade can make standard provisions for all of these conditions, but the internals of an auto trade method should be able to be tweaked in order to address some of these conditions. Our EminiScalp Pilot has provisions built in whereas a trader is able to set specific parameters for a chosen market. The previous requirement mentioned are not only important to know for auto trading, they absolutely necessary for anyone who trades manually.

The markets do the same thing all day long, every day. They react to news, they trend either up or down and they go flat at times. The only factor that may change is the number where these things take place. I feel that many traders are overwhelmed with a lot of jargon and lingo which can cause confusion. Low volume pockets, change of polarity , a responsive long or short, the market is building structure, net positive buying or selling, watch for commercial capping, now we are accepting value, market rotation within the structure, the market is coiling, and so on and on. These are items that a struggling trader should not have to think about or need to have an understanding of, at least in the beginning, if at all. I have been trading for quite a while and I really I don't see all of this as being necessary. This can only confuse a trader and may create an impression that trading will be impossible if all of this is not mastered.

Some traders may do well with all of this information, but in reality most traders do not. So, what should a trader know and what should a trader focus on in order to be a successful trader? I have my own beliefs, some of which I will write about in this article. Of course, successful trading depends quite a bit on the individual. Just because one person does well does not mean another will. Screen time, focus, learning capabilities, emotions and personality are very important factors. A setup may show on the chart and a profit target is in sight. One trader will be quick in entering, without any reservation. Another trader may hesitate, resulting in a late entry. Another trader may freeze and not enter at all. They all saw the same thing and the results were different. The price moves to the target area and the trader who did not hesitate realizes profit. For whatever reason, the other two traders had entry issues. The late entry trader either may have been stopped or realized minimal profit or a loss. The frozen trader now notices the potential profit and is annoyed that he or she was unable to enter. The last two traders are now feeling unwelcomed emotions and this will probably have a bearing on future trades.

I believe that a trader must reduce the overload and focus on what is really essential and realize that the market does three things, it goes up, down and flat. The market is also based on logic. Yes, **LOGIC**. There is no question that many will disagree with this perspective. But since most traders are not successful, it may be a good idea for these traders to look at the market in a different perspective. I am not writing this to be controversial. The market is driven by people and people have trading habits, and these habits create a trading environment. Since I believe the market does pretty much the same thing each day, I see this as being a logical trading environment. For example, there will be those traders who will trade the news. Most news driven information usually takes place at 10:00AM eastern. We know this because there is a schedule. News can be scheduled for any time, but it is not, it is scheduled for 10:00AM. So, to expect news at this time on news days is logical. Other than something unexpected, news will generally happen at 10:00AM. What is illogical are those unskilled traders who may enter a trade at this time, but we all know this does happen. Once the news comes out, the price may move wildly, either up or down. Traders will be scrambling to enter and to exit. This behavior may result in chaotic price movement. But, the market is not chaotic, it is normal because this movement is expected because it happens consistently. What seems illogical price movement is really logical price movement because the trading habits of people are causing all of this.

A prudent trader will wait until the dust settles and realize that price, in most cases, will attempt to return from where it started. This is one of my trading principles, and it is logical. This type of price movement does not only happen during news, it happens subtly all day long. A trader just has to be familiar with his or her market and stay focused.

I am not saying that all of this is easy, because it is not. The above was just an example. A trader should, in my humble opinion, decide what he or she really wants out of a trade. Logically, it is profit. Why else enter a trade. I hear all too often that the goal of trading is to preserve capital. No, the goal of trading is to INCREASE your capital. Otherwise, why bother trading. I have also been part of webinar trading competitions where the winner was the trader who lost the least amount of money. In my way of thinking, profit is the goal and if there is no profit, there is no winner.

It is imperative that a trader who wants success must approach trading in a more simplistic manner. Firstly, understand market movement in the respect that the price goes up, down and sometimes flat. That is all it does. Price should be the focus, not an indicator. Once that is understood, then a trader needs to only look for two things: the entry and the exit. The market creates both, not any method. This is where screen time is imperative. By watching numerous charts, a trader may never notice the critical trade areas.

There is really no focus and all this "confirmation" may result in missed trades and late entries.

Of course, if a trader were able to easily determine entry and target areas, then trading would be that much easier. Once a trader understands that the market creates these areas, then the road to trading success can become a reality. Two EMA's crossing or a CCI line crossing 0 may enter you in a trade after the main move has already been made. The entry may also be very close to a market created target area, which may result in a stop. This is why it is important, again in my opinion, to focus on one chart. Earlier I made mention of the goal of trading. The goal is profit, profit on each trade, profit at the end of the day, profit at the end of the week, and so on. But we all know that this is just not working for the majority of traders. It does not seem as though much progress has been made over the years in regard to the success ratio of traders. I have written about this numerous times in my book, on my website at **www.EminiScalp.com** as well as in various articles, so I won't go into much detail here. I can only theorize that with all the new methods introduced over the years, they still are saying the same thing, just packaged differently. When a trader uses a method or system where the focus is on an indicator and not on price, the results will be as they always have been.

Please understand that there are some very successful traders who use indicators. I am referring to the well over 90% who struggle to find consistency and success in their trading. Many of these successful traders built up their accounts over time and began modestly. This is the way to approach trading. Getting back to the one chart method, it may be beneficial to focus on one chart, possibly a 1 minute or a 144 tick chart. Just watch this chart every day and see what price does at certain areas. Notice where price reverses and where it goes before it reverses again. For instance, even though the trend may be up and a trader may be looking for long entries, short trades are certainly possible as well. Price will not generally move up without pullbacks.

If you watch this chart day after day and make note of what happens and where it happens, you just may observe some type of price bar or candle consistency. Knowing where to enter and where targets are is key. If traders had this information, most would be successful. Trading one or two contracts for a few ticks is a start. It certainly would be great to grab 2 or 3 ES points on each trade, but realistically this is probably not going to happen for the struggling trader, at least consistently. When SIM trading, this may be fine because a trader may let the price go against him or her more than they would normally. Enter on a real trade, and the trader gets so nervous that they can't wait to get out. The price moves one tick against the trader and a knot forms in the stomach. Not knowing market made entries and exits will doom a trader.

I have a few items in my arsenal that may help. The EminiScalp Intervals is a projective study that plots critical trade areas. If the bars or candles setup according to our method at these levels, we look for an entry. The EminiScalp Intervals also give us a nice indication of where the targets may be. This is discussed on the Eminiscalp Interval page of our website. Our ATA method will place a dot at these critical areas alerting the trader to a possible entry. Just because we have an ATA dot or a set up at the EminiScalp Interval areas does not necessarily mean that we have an entry. We need a target. If we are unable to determine a target area or if the target looks to be too close to the entry, we do not take the trade. Over time and with focus and screen time, a trader just may be able to trade without these training wheels. Just because two lines cross does not mean there is an entry. This type of trading does not take into account the true entry and target areas. This is just the way it is. Start small, take time to learn the craft, work on controlling emotions and give the method the time it deserves. Trading is not an overnight process, it takes time and continuous learning. To say "I have traded for 10 years and I have paid my dues" is not enough. If you have been looking at the wrong stuff square one is where you may need to go.

Below I have included three screen shot samples of an NQ chart. The first shows just the price candles, the second will have the EminiScalp Intervals shown and the third has the ATA added.

You will notice in the first screen shot the cycle and pullback areas. Where are the entry areas?

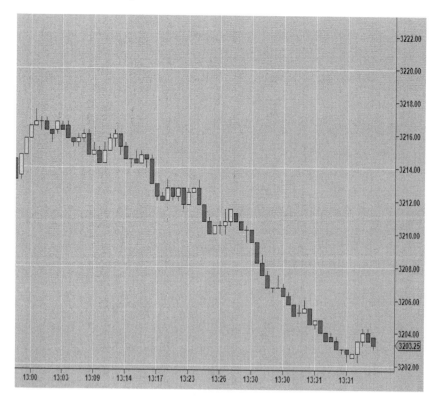

The following screen shot has the ATA added. The entry, if taken, would be on the bar following the ATA dot. The ATA documentation explains how to take entries when a dot appears. The color of the ATA dot is irrelevant, as the target and ATA dot location determine where the entry may be. A trader who uses the ATA has the option of changing the dot color as well changing the dot to another configuration such as an arrow, square, etc. Normally a green dot would indicate a long and a red dot a short, as this is usually the case.

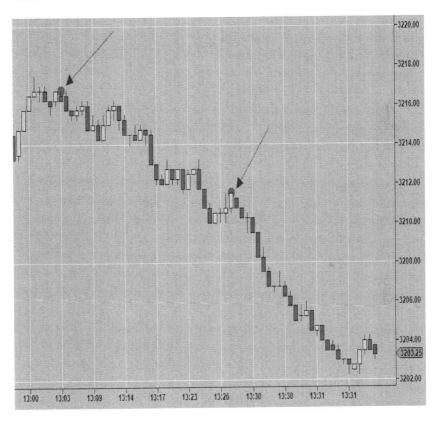

In the picture that follows, we have added the EminiScalp Intervals. Please note where price is in relation to them. In most instances, the EminiScalp Intervals are placed **well before** price reaches them. A good example of this is shown at the second blue arrow. Notice how the price reacts at the EminiScalp Intervals. Using the ATA with the EminiScalp Intervals can assist a trader in identifying trade set up areas, especially when used with our LTD method.

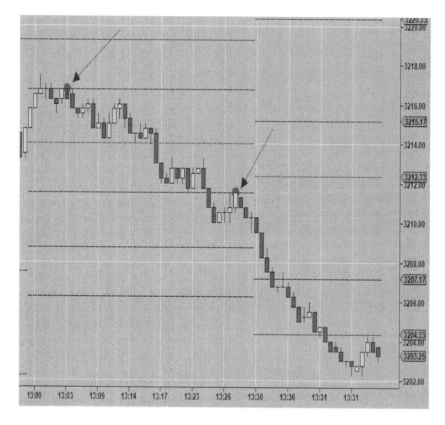

Information regarding our LTD, EminiScalp Intervals and the ATA, can be found on our website at **www.EminiScalp.com**. The EminiScalp Intervals are included with all of our methods.

Trading success is not impossible although it may seem that way. Try and keep the process simple by reducing the overload and keep in mind that trading is about entries and targets. Screen time is absolutely essential; there is no way around this.

Dual Look Back Momentum Reversals with Time and Price Strategies by Robert Miner

Dual Look Back (DLB) Momentum Reversal setups are one of the best filters to help identify high probability, low risk trade setups. If a trade is in an extreme Dual Look Back Momentum setup, the price, time and pattern position are considered to determine if the market meets all critical criteria for a specific trade strategy. The strategies taught here are applicable to any market and any time frame.

What is a Dual Look Back (DLB) Momentum Reversal setup? Most momentum indicators represent the same thing - the rate-of-change (ROC) of the trend. Momentum cycles to not represent price cycles. Momentum cycles represent the speeding up or slowing down of the trend itself.

The key variable for any momentum indicator is the look back period. With a relatively short look back period, the indicator will be very sensitive to minor momentum changes. A longer look back should be less sensitive but may lag price reversals. No one look back period will be ideal for all momentum cycle conditions. But, by understanding the position of a market from two look back periods, a trader has a higher probability of identifying an actual price reversal.

The basic strategy of the Dual Look back Momentum Reversal setups is when both look back periods are at an extreme, either overbought (OB) or oversold (OS), a market is at or very near a price high or low. When the shorter look back indicator makes a Bear or Bull Reversal while the longer look back is OB or OS, it is the final DLB setup for a momentum reversal. The price, time and pattern position will determine if the momentum reversal should coincide with a price reversal.

The indicator window in **Chart #1** shows the position of both the 13.. and 21.. DTosc momentum indicator. We have found the DTosc which is unique to our Dynamic Trader Software to be the best indicator to identify momentum trends and reversals. The 13.. look back is the shorter and 21... look back is the longer period for this example. I am using this example because we showed this exact information and the specific trade strategy in our DT Reports video in "real time".

CHART #1

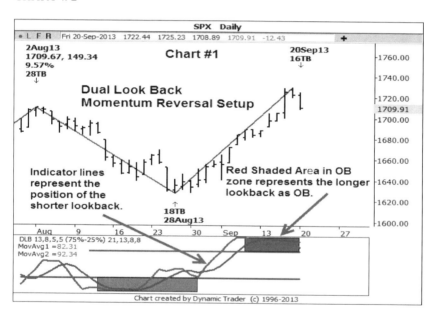

The red shaded area in the OB zone represents when fast line of the longer look back period (21..) is overbought. The indicator lines themselves represent the shorter (13..) look back indicator fast and slow lines. When the fast line crosses below the slow line the indicator has made a **Bear Reversal**.

The longer look back fast line reached the OB zone on Sept. 12, but it was not until Sept. 20 that the shorter look back made a Bear Reversal to complete the **Dual Look back Momentum Reversal** setup. Once the DLB setup is made we look at the price, time and pattern position to determine if a price reversal is likely to coincide with the momentum reversal and the specific trade strategy to enter the market.

Chart #2 shows the key time and price resistance exactly when the S&P made the DLB Momentum reversal to confirm a price reversal was also likely. The Sept. 19 high was made right in the 1723-1733 resistance price zone which included the 127% External Retracement and the 61.8% Alternate Price Projection. **Resistance Price Zones** are where several internal, symmetrical price projections are within a narrow range. Most importantly, they are known in advance so a trader is prepared for probable reversal ahead of time.

CHART #2

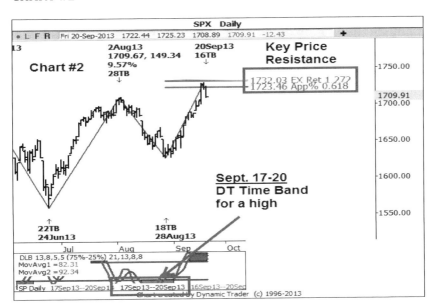

Best Trading Strategies

Sept. 17-20 was the **DT Time Band** for a high. DT Time Bands are also projected well in advance. They represent the overlap of the high – high and low – high ranges of the recent momentum and price cycles.

The setup is complete. The Dual Lookback Momentum reversal was made with price directly in the Price Resistance Zone within the DT Time Band. The next thing is to determine the specific trade strategy. My recommendation is to always let the market take you into the trade by taking out a minor swing low or a trailing one-bar-low. Ideal low risk setups are made on a shorter time frame than the trading time frame so let's take a look at the 60 minute data as of the time of the setup on Sept. 20.

Chart #3 is 60 minute data through Sept. 20. As of mid-day Sept. 20, the S&P had potentially made a simple ABC correction. The Wave-1 minor swing low was the prior day's low. The entry strategy is to go short one tick below the trailing daily one bar low (the probable W.1 minor swing low) with an initial stop one tick above the recent minor swing high.

CHART #3

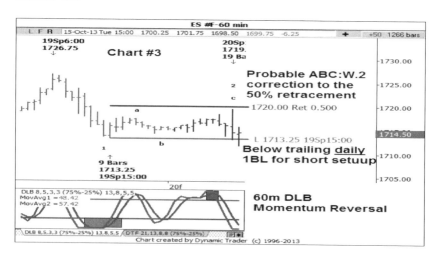

The short trade was made at 1713.00 with a stop at 1719.50. The entry and initial stop prices are always known in advance so the trader can determine the position size before the trade is entered. Traders can choose to short futures or a bear ETF with 2 or 3 times leverage that takes advantage of a down market.

This example has only demonstrated the setup conditions for a trade and the specific entry strategy. It does not address how the trade is then managed until the exit strategy including the stop loss adjustments as the trend progresses.

The Dual Look Back Momentum setup with price, time and pattern position strategies are used with any market and any time frame from day trades to multi-week position trades. We describe the setups daily in our DT Daily Reports for day and swing traders and the DT Just-In-Time and DT Alert Reports intermediate to position trades.

For a comprehensive education of the complete trade strategies from entry to exit, see Robert Miner's most recent book, *High Probability Trade Strategies* available with a 2-hour video CD from www.DynamicTraders.com.

THE A-B-C PRICE PULSE – TRADING THE C WAVE BY JACK CROOKS

Trading for real money isn't easy. But one of the lessons I've learned over the years is we tend to make trading harder than it should be. I am going to share a simplified pattern analysis approach that I apply every day in my currency trading and newsletter service--trading the C-Wave..

It is too clear and so it is hard to see.

A dunce searched for fire with a lit lantern.

Had he known what fire was he would have cooked his rice sooner.

The Gateless Gate

I have experimented with many different technical analysis tools and trading techniques over the last 25-years of trading; ranging from old school point and figure charting to new world computer algorithms. But given how I personally process and absorb market information I have learned pattern analysis (or pattern recognition) works best for me. *[One of your primary goals as a trader is to find what best works for you.].*

The particular style of analysis I now employ, for lack of a better term, is a modified form of Elliott Wave (EW) analysis. But instead of worrying too much about the plethora of rules and searching for the perfect textbook stylized wave pattern, I keep it simple.

I refer to my simple approach to pattern analysis as looking for three-wave pulse price action--A-B-C or 1-2-3. It works in all time frames. This new way of seeing has helped me identify more high probability trade setups; and has improved my win:loss ratio and risk management.

I have been studying and applying EW analysis to market trading decisions across a host of different asset classes over the past twenty years. Attempting to define the perfect stylized EW pattern in price action too often proved frustrating and elusive. Often I would be on the right track in recognizing an excellent trading setup, only to be foiled by one of the many rules embedded in the EW system. In retrospect I was missing the forest for the trees.

There were two primary problems I kept running up against as I attempted to a strict EW approach:

1. **I kept seeing impulse moves with three wave instead of five.** In EW parlance, the market moves in five waves impulse waves [defining the direction of the primary trend], then corrects in three waves [against the primary trend]. <u>I kept having trouble with that pesky fifth wave of an impulse move that was supposed to form.</u>

2. **The overlap rule in EW.** One of the unbreakable rules of EW analysis is that a fourth wave cannot penetrate into the territory of the first wave of the same degree [except for a well-defined pattern exception]. Attempting to apply this iron clad EW rule forced me to miss many excellent trade setups.

Therefore I decided to focus on the three-wave price pulse and no longer worry about the EW overlap rule...simple! Well, at least it made it a lot easier and has paid dividends.

So let me give you an example of "seeing in threes"...instead of five; then give you some basic guidelines so you can give this simple but naturally powerful approach a try in your own trading...

Standardized Elliott Five Wave Price Pattern vs. Modified Three Wave Pulse A-B-C

Elliott vs. Modified Wave Structure

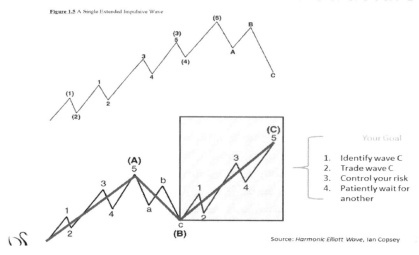

Source: *Harmonic Elliott Wave*, Ian Copsey

Okay. That is the basic framework. Now let's take a look at some FX price charts in three different time frames--USD/CAD Daily, AUD/USD Weekly, and USD/JPY Hourly. In each series the chart only first, then the chart with the three wave price pulse highlighted...

USD/CAD Daily
Sight Recognition?

Speakers of Traders World Online Expo #14

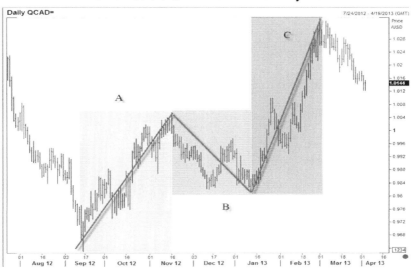

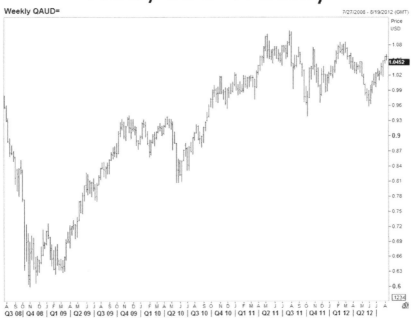

Best Trading Strategies

A-B-C AUD/USD

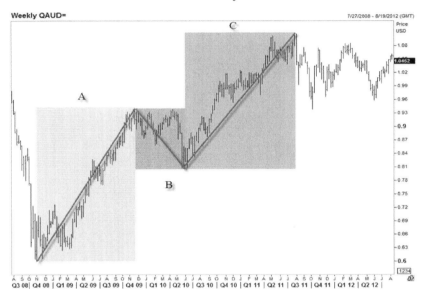

A-B-C Pattern

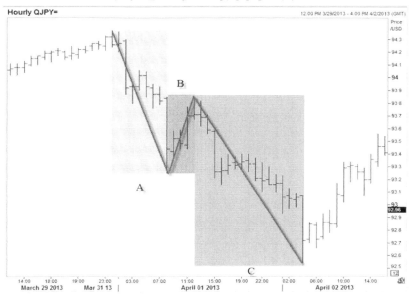

You will be very surprised how quickly you begin to visualize these patterns in many of the charts where you haven't seen them before, now that you know what to look for. It is the beginning of your pattern recognition trading...all it takes is an open mind and a little practice.

Now, go back and look at the three examples again. Think about the A-B-C. Now, you need only a few additional elements to the equation to help you better identify each of the waves and the ultimate trading setup--Wave C:

Identify the **Swing High (or low)** as the beginning reference for Wave A. In the example below--AUD/USD Weekly--the swing low was near 0.6000 back in Q$ of 2008; that was the start of Wave-A for analysis purposes.

Overlay the **Fibonacci retracement levels** to help project and identify the end of Wave B - this is CRITICAL: I recommend you wait for Wave B to retrace at least 38% of Wave A before considering it complete and the Wave C is about to begin. You may miss some trades because of this, but more often than not I have noticed when Wave B retracements are less than 38.2% of Wave A, subsequent rallies were often head fakes. See the example below:

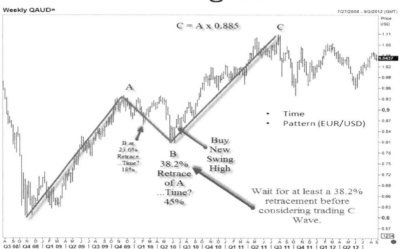

The initial pull-back into Wave B was 23.6%; then the move up was a rally above the swing high--this was an example of a head fake, as Wave B eventually retraced 38.2% of Wave A. At that point it represented a much higher probability setup to suggest Wave C was about to begin. The entry point was a break above the minor swing high near 0.8400; Wave C rallied all the way to 1.1100 before ending.

Though not critical, but it does provide some additional clues, you can apply **Relative Price Index (RSI)** to wave B looking for "overbought" or "oversold" or price divergences--if these coincide with a key Fibonacci retracement level, it adds credence that Wave B may be completing and Wave C may soon begin.

From a tactical standpoint, **you can use the various minor swing high and swing low levels as stop-loss points once you enter the trade.** See the example below again looking at AUD/USD Weekly. In this example the stop-loss was adjusted upward 5 times after the initial stop-loss was set at the swing low. Then the trade was finally stopped out with approximately 1,200 pips per contract (on a regular sized contract in retail forex that would represent about $12,000 per contract profit):

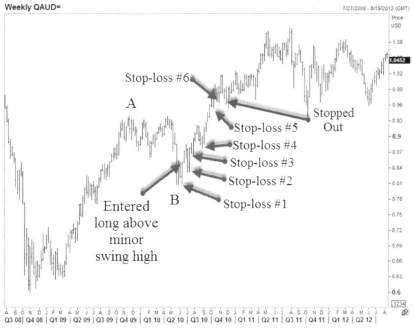

As you become more adept at seeing the three wave price pulses, what happens next is **you will often start seeing three waves nested inside the larger A-B-C wave.** Take a look at the example below of USD/JPY in the 10-min time frame (the same 3-3-3 pattern tends to show up often across all time frames--it is fractal):

A-B-C (10-min of prior)
3-3-3

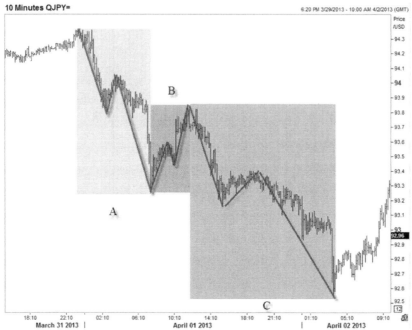

Is trading Wave C perfect? Of course not! But if applied correctly, it will allow you to identify high probability trade setups, and using near-term swing low/high areas for controlling risk and locking in profit. In short you have all the elements you need to ride a trend and make money. What more can we ask for.

Jack Crooks

Black Swan Capital

www.blackswantrading.com

jcrooks@blackswantrading.com

Without these 2 Important Keys, You Will Fail in Trading by Ken W. Chow

You want to trade successfully to earn a steady income. But have you ever looked carefully at what is really required to make and keep money over time?

There are 2 important parts needed to win consistently. Both of these two components are absolutely necessary for maintaining long term profitability. You are doomed to failure if you don't have both.

The first part is…

Outer Game

What is outer game?

In sports, it's the proper techniques. It's the correct way to perform a golf swing, or a good throwing form in football.

In trading, it's having a solid trading methodology. It is absolutely necessary that it gives you an edge. Without it, you'll find it's impossible to win.

There are many trading techniques that can make money for a trader.

Personally, I use clustering extreme Fibonacci numbers with lots of confirmation for entering a trade. Price charts give me a clear visual map of the market without the clutter of indicators. Chart patterns clearly show me increasing or decreasing trend strength as the market unfolds. I found a method that makes sense to me.

Does the trading approach you're using fit your own particular trading style? Do you lean on indicators to flash trade setups, or do you prefer to read charts like I do? Are you more comfortable interpreting news and government reports to make trading decisions?

These are important questions to address before proceeding to trade. If you're wondering whether you should use all the methods I mentioned, you will be confused and overwhelmed.

Why? Because there are times when they are in conflict. Better to pick an approach that fits your trading style and not try to cover too many bases. You'll go crazy processing too much information.

Are you a short term or long term trader?

Are you able to withstand wild overnight swings using wider protective stops? Are you comfortable taking fewer trades per month? If so, swing or position trading will be right for you.

If you want to end your trading day flat the market, and don't mind watching every tick when trading, then day trading would work well for you.

By understand your own trading style, you feel less stressed when entering and managing your trades.

Once you've decided on the actual tools that you use to trade, you should understand all the "moving parts" and nuances of your trading method. Knowing all the strengths and weaknesses allow you to formulate practical rules to follow.

There are many trading systems out there. You can purchase someone else's or devise one yourself. Either way, get one that fits your personality and get to know it inside out.

Inner Game

An even more important aspect of trading is what's known as inner game. Without it, you will struggle to maintain profitability.

Inner game is defined as your concentration, your confidence, and your mental toughness you bring to any task. In trading, it's been said that the mental/emotional aspect to trading contributes to 80% of what's needed to win, while the actual trading technique only amounts to the remaining 20%.

In sports, all the greatest champions have super strong inner game. Michael Jordan is known for his mental toughness as his athletic ability. Tiger Woods has seen his fantastic inner game in golf deteriorate after losing focus due to the public exposure of his marital affairs.

Every time you enter a trade, you are competing against the brightest minds in the world. Smart professional traders from large banks and other institutions may be taking the other side of your position. Yes, you can take your share of the profits, but you need to bring a strong inner constitution to compete in the market.

I will point out a few things I do regularly to constantly improve my inner game.

Stress Reduction

First and foremost, we need to address the stress in our daily lives.

We all experience tremendous physical and psychological stress in today's world. As traders, stress can destroy a trading account mercilessly and bring on unnecessary agony. When stressed, we all make silly mistakes. We do not act in our best interest.

Since we are trading against the most brilliant professionals in the world that are out to get our hard-earned money, we need to approach the market in the best shape possible. Neutralizing stress on a regular basis is the first order of business.

Get in the best physical shape possible. Intense physical exercise has shown to benefit both the body and the brain. By pumping an increased supply of oxygen into circulation, we can process trading data clearly and calmly with an improved brain.

I also do stretching and yoga movements for flexibility. We need to be flexible not just physically but also mentally, which is crucial for making quick trading decisions.

Get off your chair every half hour or so and move around. This helps circulation of the blood and the lymphatic system.

Of course, do eat wholesome nutritious food and drink plenty of good water. Reduce or eliminate junk food, alcohol, and sugar from your diet. They put unwanted stress inside the organs of your body.

High quality vitamins and minerals are the essential foundation that must be taken by everyone. Make sure you also take quality fish oil to improve brain function.

After getting the proper exercises and food, do whatever you can to relax as much as possible. Get plenty of sleep to be fully rested. Meditate to keep the mind and spirit sharp. Pamper yourself with a soothing massage every week or so.

Breathing exercises are powerful for reducing stress. One of my favorite is alternate nostril breathing. It's very effective for balancing the left and right hemispheres of the brain. It only takes 5 minutes to perform.

Other brain specific exercises are very helpful when done on a regular basis.

There are simple exercises such as 'balancing the cortices' and 'super brain yoga' that only take a couple of minutes to perform. All this information is free. You can google these techniques for more information.

I know all this sounds like health advice. I am not a health professional. I'm just sharing my own experience here. Do consult your doctor. I

Resolving Deep Psychological Issues

If you take an honest evaluation of your psychological make-up, can you identify areas that can use improvement?

Trading is the best business in the world because you have complete freedom to do whatever you want. Enter or exit the market at any price and anytime. You answer to no boss or customers. In the end, it's just you and your mental makeup that confronts the market. And you bring all your unresolved problems to trading.

In teaching traders my methodology over the years, many of my own students out trade me on a regular basis. The one thing they all have something in common is they naturally have balanced happy mental makeup.

Do you lack discipline? Are you impatient? Are you fearful? Do you have negative self-talk and beliefs? These and other disempowering issues are so deeply rooted in our subconscious that we may have forgotten about them. Many of them are from our childhood.

At work or in social situations, we can mask these personal demons to accomplish the task at hand. We can use lame excuses or workarounds as a temporary fix.

But in trading, you cannot hide from yourself. You express your deepest psychological issues when you trade. In fact, a price chart is simply a graphical depiction of all the traders participating in that market expressing their fear and greed collectively.

These buried issues come pouring out when a trading decision needs to made, resulting in a profit or loss. You must neutralize them before you can be consistently profitable.

What can we do to uproot these difficult issues?

I have personally tried all types of self-improvement modalities. Many only scratch the surface. Motivational CDs and workshops can pump you up temporarily, but fade just as quickly.

Flower Essences?

This one healing approach is very unusual. I won't be surprised if you decide to skip this section. However, I found that using flower essences to be the most powerful and very easy to apply. They are very inexpensive as well.

In the 1930's, Dr. Edward Bach discovered 38 different flower essences that address 38 corresponding negative emotions that are common in people all over the world. You may be currently suffering from a handful of these bothersome issues.

Each flower essence can reverse specific character flaws a person may be carrying, sometime for decades. This healing system can work for anyone without having them dig up and analyze a negative issue. Just identify the issue and take the specific flower essence to eliminate it. This clearing process may take days, weeks or months.

There is one for fear, another for confidence, etc. Google Bach Flower Essences to find out more.

Trading coaches

Trading coaches are professionals who specialize in helping traders become more successful by overcoming their perceived limitations. They can be very valuable for improving your trading results. However, I suggest hiring one only after you've done everything to improve yourself as mentioned above.

You first need to lay the groundwork for their techniques to stick. Having a healthy body and mind goes a long way for taking advantage of their work. Otherwise, any coaching would just be layered superficially on top of your unresolved personal issues, and won't help you in the long run

In summary, consistently successful trading requires a sound trading methodology. However, you need to make constant improvement to your body and mind in order to apply your tools for maximum effectiveness and sustained profitability.

A strong inner game cannot be overstated. Take care of yourself as best as you can, so you can bring a powerful mind to your trading. In the end, trading is all "mind".

Having a calm, clear, focused subconscious mind free of internal conflicts will allow you to consistently apply your trading rules properly. As a side benefit, you will also live a much happier life to enjoy your trading profits.

For more information go to: www.SuperStructureTrading.com

The Market Profile™ Graph and and How to Trade It by Tom Alexander

Market Profile™ Graph Basics

The traditional Market Profile™ graphic uses letters to depict the vertical range of each specific thirty-minute time period in a trading, or auction, unit (the day session of the stock index futures, for instance). The trading session of a given asset is divided into thirty-minute time periods with each time period being assigned a letter. The initial instance the market trades at a price a letter designated for that thirty-minute period is placed on the chart. Only one letter per time period will print regardless of how many instances price trades at that level within the thirty-minute period. When the thirty-minute period completes the next time period begins as the chart shifts one column to the right and the letter designation changes. Another way of stating this is that each letter is basically a thirty-minute bar, but instead of a straight line the bar is a vertical line of a single letter representing a designated time period. The chart below (fig. 1) illustrates the S&P mini futures day session which has a 15-minute period from 4:00-4:15, and that time period is designated by the letter "P".

Speakers of Traders World Online Expo #14

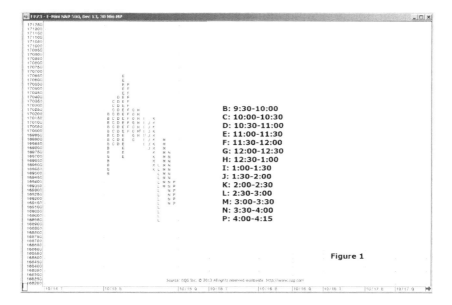

Figure 1

Below (fig. 2) is the same chart above but in the traditional Market Profile™ view.

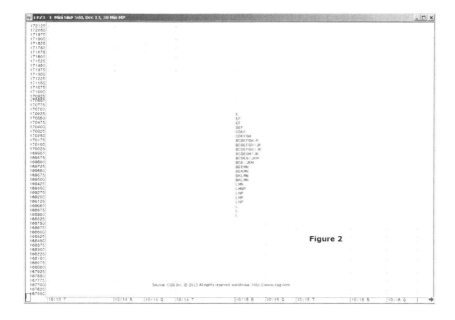

Figure 2

The letters used to designate the trading activity are referred to as TPOs, which stands for Time Price Opportunity (per Steidlmayer), or That Price Occurred (per Jones). A TPO signifies that a market traded at least once at a specific price within that designated time period. A profile's rotations, or designated time periods can be any length of time. We quite often look at daily profiles where each letter will represent one day's trading. Because Market Development and Market Structure occur in all degrees of time all the time, the same objective analysis can be applied in the timeframe most useful to the individual trader. A very important point is that regardless of the timeframe one chooses to trade, all the way down to the very short-term daytrader, because the processes of Market Development and Market Structure are occurring across all timeframes all the time, the context of the present phase of development within the larger phases of development can provide a huge edge, and is one of the primary benefits of using this methodology as a model to develop a trading plan.

Two legacy components of the traditional Market Profile™ chart are the Initial Balance period and the Value Area. The Initial Balance Period is the range of the first two half-hour periods of the trading day or session for that particular contract. The Initial Balance Period was extremely important in the early days of Market Profile™. It was used to help define potential range as well as help identify when the institutions or other big money participants (often referred to as "other timeframe players") were initiating positions. The theory was that most of the range in the first hour of trading was determined by the floor traders. If the floor was in control of the market the range would be relatively narrow and there would not be much extension outside of the first hour range. Because floor traders had negligible transaction costs and could make money while price stayed in a relatively narrow controlled range, there was no incentive for range extension as long as the floor traders were in control of the marketplace. If the range suddenly extended outside the range of the first hour it was most often because the off floor traders of institutions were imitating positions and their size would push the market directionally outside the range of the first hour of trading, or Initial Balance Period. The amount of buying or selling the off floor trader conducted during the day would determine the form of one of several typical Market Profile™ day-type patterns. It is important to note that in Market Profile™ literature through the mid 1990's the Market Profile™ concept emphasized each day as a discreet event, but one that had predictive value regarding near term market direction based on an interpretation of the particular day type that was formed. This has been proven to be a flawed concept and the use and value of the Market Profile™ has evolved dramatically over the past fifteen years.

The highest use of the Market Profile™ graph is to use it is a tool to analyze markets through the lens of *Auction Market Principles*. Used this way, the Market Profile™ graph becomes an extraordinarily consistent and objective way of determining potential support and resistance areas, which we refer to as Key Reference Areas (KRAs). KRAs provide an inherent trading edge in that they are inflection points from where markets are more likely than random to begin a sharp trend.

One of the obvious differences between a Market Profile™ chart and a bar chart is the information that is available on the horizontal scale of the chart. It is easier to see the *amount of activity that occurred at a given price or area of prices* on a Market Profile™ chart than a bar chart. As we will explain in detail later, this is a critical and defining difference.

Benefits of the Market Profile™ Graphing Format

Because of the way the MP Graph organizes data, the auction process that drives all auction markets (all electronic markets are "auction" markets) is displayed in a consistent manner that highlights the recurring patterns of the development process of an auction. This process is remarkably robust and therefore the patterns are remarkably consistent. The most recognizable pattern is that of the bell-shaped curve standing on edge. This pattern occurs in all time frames and in all markets, which gives those that have a thorough understanding knowledge of the MP Graph and the development phases of an auction that are driving the trade activity a huge edge. This "look" is consistent across timeframes and different markets because the auction process is the same across all timeframes and all markets. It is the most logical and objective way possible to analyze a market.

The consistency of this process provides the background in developing a consistent trading plan that is as objective as a discretionary model can possibly be.

The Three-Step Auction Process

The Auction Market Development Process begins with a "Mature Auction", which is an auction that is about to transition into another "auction". Below (fig. 3) is a profile graph of Wal-Mart stock that depicts a mature auction from January-October 2009.

Speakers of Traders World Online Expo #14

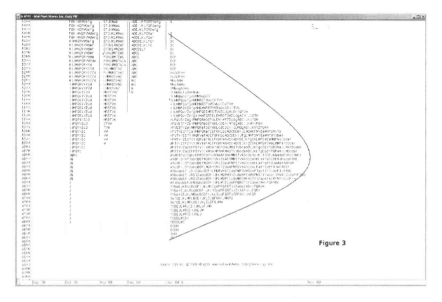

Below (fig. 4) is a Step 1 as Wal-Mart begins to transition from one auction to another.

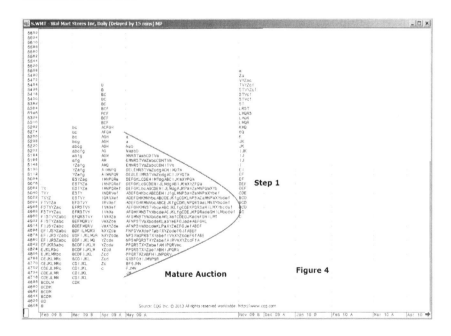

Best Trading Strategies

Step 2 (fig. 5) is the development phase in which the auction finds and accepts a new level of relative value, around which it trades from its upper to lower extremes.

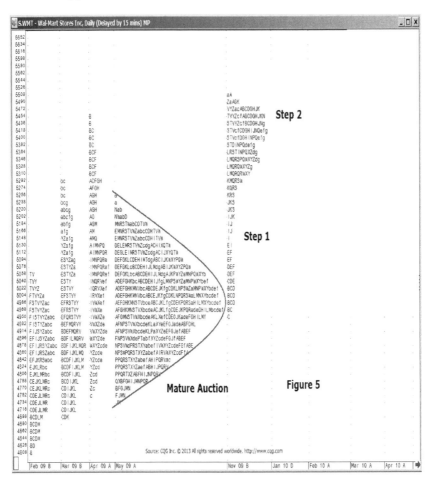

Figure 5

Step 3 (fig. 6) brings the market into another state of Mature Balance and the process will inevitable begin again. *This process is in effect in all degrees of time all the time in all markets.*

Speakers of Traders World Online Expo #14

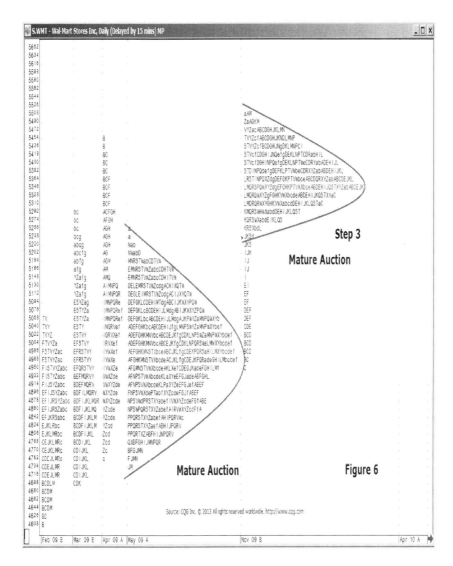

This process consistently creates three distinct areas (Key Reference Areas) that provide a trading edge (fig. 7)

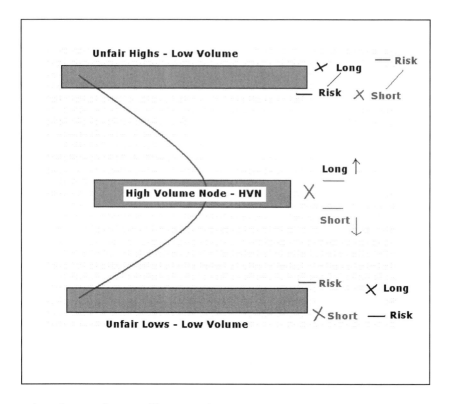

What the Market Profile™ Graphing Format IS NOT

The MP Graph is not magic. It is not a trading system; it is a specific way of organizing price data that helps identify the most productive areas, and times, to trade. It does not relieve the trader from having to work or think. It can bring consistency, objectivity logic and rigor to a trading methodology and that is a LOT!

My book, *Practical Trading Applications of Market Profile*, can be purchased on Amazon:

http://www.amazon.com/Practical-Trading-Applications-Market-Profile/dp/0615300464

The Simplest Proven Day Trading Method with a Track Record by Gerard P. Reynaud

Trading is by far one of the hardest activities that any human being could attempt to become successful at. The good news is that successful trading is possible. But while many programs focus on setup and pattern recognition along with signals, indicators and other 'timing' factors, successful trading is achieved only by being able to maintain a solid action plan. Being a disciplined trader means checking your emotions at the door and practicing to get good at it. In my early trading days, I used to feel very challenged when I was told to not become emotional. Hey! I'm only human… How could I not become emotional?

On any given trading day, everything will start developing rather quickly. Before you can even think of pulling the trigger, first you have to make sure that you have truly checked two of the hardest emotions to combat at the door, anxiety and desperation. First rule of successful trading is waiting for the setup to fully develop according to your guidelines. When you are ready to pull the trigger and the magical moment of getting filled rings the mighty chime, there are many possible scenarios that may affect the outcome of the trade. Here are some of the most common ones about how we usually react (we are all humans, right?) and what we should do instead after getting filled:

Trade is going your direction: Awesome! You feel you are the king of the world. All of the sudden you get greedy and move your target to get more out of your trade… of course, you notice later that there was a great area of resistance and your long position all of the sudden gets back to breakeven of even worse, it stops you out. Avoid the temptation! If you are trading multiple contracts, get your initial target with half the number of contracts you are trading and the rest, let it run with a trailing stop. That way you are ensuring you get your profit and the rest is just the icing on the cake (which in some cases may be of great profitability). And don't forget; always look at the big picture, where areas of support and resistance may be.

You got in the trade, but the market is doing NOTHING! Yeah, you thought your long position was a great setup and all buyers were supposed to get in, right? After all now you realize -well, is it lunch hour? Or where did the volume go? The market is taking a nap and you get emotional, you want to see some action and trigger another order, just to take some ticks more out of this boring trade. Well, you should have your time stops in mind. The statistical probability of the trade moving in your favor does fade out as time elapses. Whatever the timeframe or range you are trading, it is best to GET OUT should the price action flatten or stall. Nothing else, it's like going to a boring party.

Oh sugar!... The trade is going south! You start panicking and fear will cause you to do the things that you fear the most. Now you question whether your stop may be a little too wide so you move it closer, to find out one second later -when you actually just got stopped out, of course- that the trade started going in your desired direction. How can you eliminate this emotional need to "protect yourself"? First, even before you get in the trade, you have to feel very comfortable with your initial stop, assuming that's a risk you and your portfolio are able to take, otherwise you are sabotaging yourself from the beginning and you will not be able to let the trade work! Let it breathe... now, always pay attention to where your stops are, let's suppose your rules say that your stop should be 10 ticks below your entry, but your stop could then be sitting right on an MA, a Fib retracement, a round number or at another significant level of support or resistance... then you may need to adjust slightly.

The probabilities of getting stopped out at one of these levels is certainly higher. If you realize by moving your stop that your risk is greater than what you can afford, then don't take the trade altogether. Wait for another setup that has all the right conditions and reasons to get in. Ultimately controlling anxiety and desperation will keep you one step ahead of the game.

So even though we may be tempted by our emotions, we need to train ourselves to avoid these very natural and common mistakes. A great way to identify how your emotions are getting on your way, is to set the action plan and keep a journal. I know that keeping a journal sounds like a teenage girl thing, but it is a must! The most important field the journal should include, is a comment box where you could write down why did you enter a trade, what setup were you looking for, what was your risk:reward and how did you manage your trade. Did you move your stop? Why? Did you exit early? Did you scale in? etc.. Then review it at night and analyze how you are reacting to these 3 scenarios. Training yourself to be disciplined will pay off at the end.

Remember that trading will require you to think –and do- opposite to everything we have been programmed as humans since birth. The reason many traders fail is not because of their system, lack of knowledge or tools. It's mainly because we were never programmed to stay cool in the face of adversity or harm. Or not caring one bit when your account faces a significant drawdown. The market will dictate how the price action develops during any given moment, but only you can dictate how you react to it.

Best way to put it, you can't control the market, you can only control yourself.

Gerard P. Reynaud, President/Founder, www.TraderMakers.com

THE PERFECT GROWTH STOCK BY ROSS GIVENS

When it comes to longer term investing, there are two primary schools of thought – growth and value. And most people believe these to be exclusive of one another. They either try to pick the next Google or buy a more predictable company when its stock price is low from a fundamental perspective.

But what if there was a combination of both? Is there such a thing? Are there stocks that have demonstrated an explosive track record of growth but also offer an ideal price based on their current levels of earnings and assets?

The answer is yes, and this is exactly the type of stock that every investor dreams of owning. Apple presented such an opportunity around the year 2000, and you don't need me to tell you how that turned out for everyone who recognized the situation. I have identified another stock available today that offers just such an opportunity. Even better, there is a free technical indicator that has consistently picked the lows of this stock for the past ten years.

To fully grasp the opportunity of this investment, it is important that you understand the broad strokes of value versus growth investing.

The concept of value is fairly simple. You want to receive lots of assets, high cash flows and a low stock price relative to both. There are several investment metrics to help identify these which include its price to earnings multiple (P/E) and price to book value (P/B). Essentially, you want to pay as little as possible for each year's earnings and the net assets, i.e. book value, of the company.

The concept of growth is fairly straight forward as well. You want a stock that is demonstrated growing revenues, increasing profits and growing or at least maintaining profit margins. After all, more sales mean nothing if it doesn't translate to higher earnings for shareholders.

The tricky part of growth investing is price. Since you are paying for what is yet to happen, the corresponding stock price is derived from a wide range of analyst expectations of what may or may not take place in the coming years. This is what makes stocks like Amazon and Tesla so risky. The company needs to not only grow, but do so at the pace forecasted by Wall Street. So even if their sales increase over the previous year, the stock price will decline if this increase falls short of expectations. In order to profit from high growth stocks, the company must exceed the metrics already priced into its shares.

The easiest way to identify value versus growth opportunities is in their earnings multiples. The P/E ratio tells you how many times last year's earnings you are paying for the stock. Value opportunities generally trade below 15, since this is a baseline metric of fair market value of any stable company. Growth stocks on the other hand can trade from 30 – 1,000 times earnings. Why? As we discussed, you are paying for what Wall Street believes the company will do in the coming years. They believe that a price of 100 times today's net income is justifiable since that figure is expected to increase dramatically going forward.

Our goal as investors should be to find the perfect combination of both – a company growing at a rate well beyond the overall market but still trading for a price that makes sense even at today's level of earnings. To find these gems, you want the following metrics to be met:

Increasing revenues and profits by at least 15% annually

P/E ratio below 15 (below 10 is ideal)

Consistently profitable track record of 5 years or more

Price/Book ratio below 3.0

Recession-proof business model

What stock fits all of these metrics today? World Acceptance Corporation (WRLD).

WRLD is a small loan consumer finance company. They offer small loans (average loan size is $1,280) to customers with subprime credit. In 2012 they grossed just over $3 billion in loan volume. Founded in 1962, they now operate 1,203 loan offices across 13 states and Mexico.

At first, a subprime lender may sound like a very risky business model. However, I do not believe this company to carry anywhere near the risk of the larger, more traditional lending institutions. This is because of their customer base and average loan size. Larger banking institutions focus on personal mortgage and business loans. This leaves them subject to economic downturns that can drastically affect their bottom line and create 2008-type disasters. Their exposure is so great that even small fluctuations in business conditions or housing prices translate into catastrophic write-downs for the lender. World Acceptance, on the other hand, is open to much less economic risk. Their customer base is already comprised of clients with subprime credit. The default risk is already underwritten into their loan portfolio and compensated for with above average interest rates. Between the 2007 economic peak and the 2009 depression, charge-offs on WRLD's books fluctuated by less than 3% of the total portfolio.

The fundamental metrics are more than adequate for this stock. It has a P/E ratio of just 12.1 and a free cash flow yield of just less than 20% (compared to roughly a 5% average for most blue chips today). The company has been profitable for the last ten years and continues to see growing revenues and profits. Earnings have been growing at an average annual rate of 15.13% for each of the last ten years. Revenues have grown an average of 14.00%. The charts below show the company's ten-year growth history.

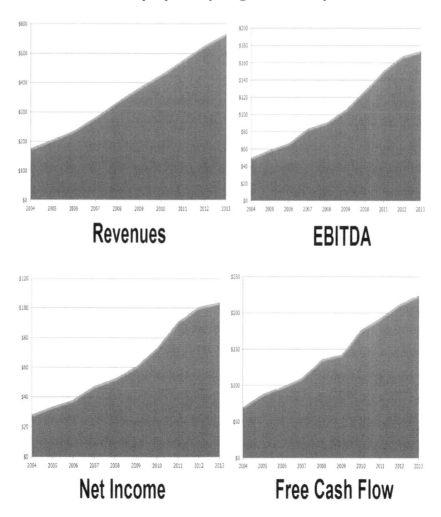

Based on the discount cash flow valuation method, this stock is wildly underpriced. If it were to grow just 10% annually for the next 10 years (compared to over 15% for the previous 10), the stock should be worth approximately $346 per share today. That is 262% above today's price of $95. Below is the breakdown of that model.

Discount Cash Flow Valuation							
10 Year Growth Rate	Terminal Growth Rate:	Initial Owner Earnings		Discount Rate			
10.00%	4.00%	$224.21		9.00%			
Change Cell	Change Cell	Default	Custom	Clear Cell			
Year	Growth Rate	Projected Owner Earnings	Present Value		PV of Future Cash Flows:		$4,273.09
2014	10.00%	$246.63	$226.27				
2015	10.00%	$271.29	$228.34		Stockholders' Equity:		
2016	10.00%	$298.42	$230.44				
2017	10.00%	$328.27	$232.55		Intrinsic Value:		$4,273.09
2018	10.00%	$361.09	$234.69				
2019	10.00%	$397.20	$236.84		# of Shares Outstanding:		12.34
2020	10.00%	$436.92	$239.01				
2021	10.00%	$480.61	$241.20		Value Per Share:		$346.28
2022	10.00%	$528.68	$243.42				
2023	10.00%	$581.54	$245.65		Margin of Safety:		50.00%
2024	4.00%	$604.80	$234.38				
2025	4.00%	$629.00	$223.63				
2026	4.00%	$654.16	$213.37		Buy Below:		$173.14
2027	4.00%	$680.32	$203.58				
2028	4.00%	$707.54	$194.25				
2029	4.00%	$735.84	$185.34				
2030	4.00%	$765.27	$176.83				
2031	4.00%	$795.88	$168.72				
2032	4.00%	$827.72	$160.98				
2033	4.00%	$860.83	$153.60				

But there are two extra kickers that make this stock even more attractive.

High Insider Ownership – 22.67% of the outstanding shares are owned by company insiders. This means that company employees have over $269 million of their own money at risk. Why is this important? It aligns the interests of executives with those of the shareholders. With so much of their personal wealth tied to the stock price, they are incentivized to take actions that will increase shareholder value.

Share Buybacks – The company has been steadily buying back shares on the open market for the past nine years. This is a double positive for us. First, it shows that the company recognizes the undervaluation of their stock. Second, stock buybacks are great for existing shareholders. Buy buying back and retiring shares, it concentrates our position. In other words, each share represents a greater percentage of the overall company. WLRD has been buying back an average of 1.1 million shares annually (9.15% of the total outstanding).

Now that you understand why this is such a valuable investment opportunity, let's look at a technical indicator that has almost perfectly picked the lows of this stock for the last decade.

The indicator I am referring to is the RSI – relative strength index. RSI is a technical momentum indicator that compares the magnitude of recent gains to losses. The result is a numeric reading between 0 and 100 representing oversold and overbought conditions. A reading below 30 is indicative of an oversold situation one above 70 is said to be overbought. While I would not recommend using this tool as your sole basis for buying and selling, it does a wonderful job of identifying opportune times to buy trending stocks.

As a longer-term trader, I prefer to use this indicator on a weekly chart using an input of 14 periods. Anything shorter than a weekly chart makes the indicator less predictable and will likely result in false signals. Only twice in the last ten years has an oversold indication on the weekly chart of WRLD not let to greater than 50% gains. Adding to one's position each time the RSI turned up from a reading below 30 for the past five years would have generated average annual returns of over 71%. The lower chart shows relative lows identified by this indicator over the last decade.

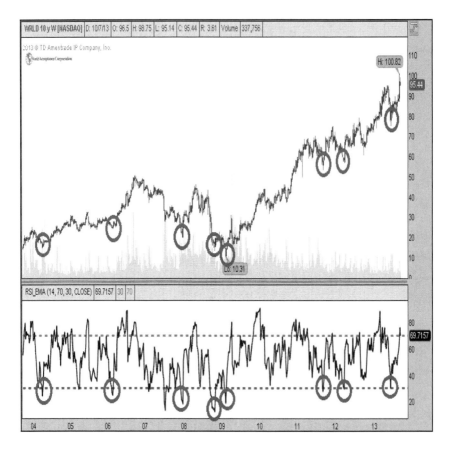

Be sure not to buy until the RSI begins to turn up. While some of the dips below 30 may be brief, others can push even further, leaving the stock in oversold territory for several weeks. Wait for the relative strength line to begin progressing higher. The charts below show two examples, one in which the oversold reading was brief and another in which the stock continued another 50% lower before the RSI turned higher.

Speakers of Traders World Online Expo #14

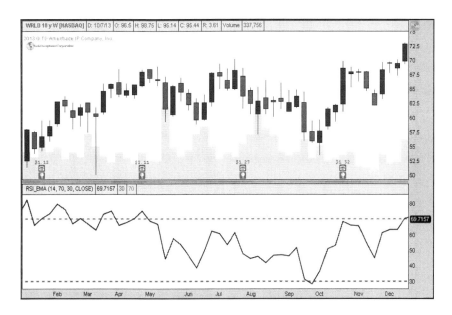

Shallow Oversold RSI Reading

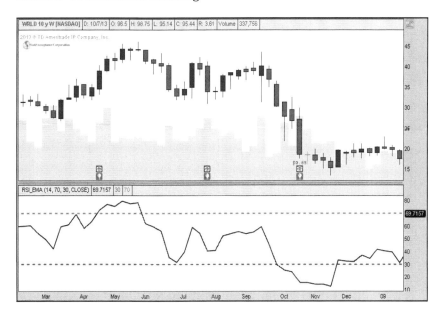

Deep Oversold RSI Reading

Technical analysis is a wonderful tool when used properly. The mistake that many traders make is relying on it fully and paying no attention to the underlying company. One should use indicators as a tool to more precisely execute fundamentally sound trades. This allows traders to leverage the buying pressure of both technical and fundamental investors.

Disclosure: Long WRLD

For more information contact Ross Givens at www.bluetickresearch.com

Harmonic Wave Convergence – The New Paradigm of Currency Trading by Steve Gregor

Who is interested in making 3X, 5X, 10X more, in the same trades, than your trading peers, or that you may be making now? That was the drive for me to discover Harmonic Wave Convergence ("HWC").

Without sounding harsh, what I am going to discuss here is not for new traders. The perfect candidate is a trader who has been trading for some time, and has not yet found their comfort with consistent trading results. In other words, they are not yet ready to trade live money, or worse, they have been trading live money and refunding their trading account because of consistent loses. The ideal candidate for my program are the traders who realize there is something very real about trading, has not achieved that reality, and is finally ready to commit to getting away from the smoke-and-mirrors used by most folks marketing strategies and systems to them. They are ready for that "come to Jesus meeting" with themselves regarding their trading.

We are not for traders that are just checking things out, looking for yet another holy grail to add to their 137 indicators they already have on their MT4 platform, or hoping to buy something on Friday and be trading it on Monday. If they haven't realized that has not already worked for them, we aren't going to be much good for them. We are ready for serious, committed, going to persist-without-exception trading students, who truly want to master the charts.

While HWC is valid on all time periods in all markets, I particularly trade just the Forex and coach traders how to trade the Forex. The years of trading, research, development, and effort have all been within the Forex market. And with the laser-precision opportunities

I have with HWC in the Forex, I've not been motivated or had the need to trade other markets. However, I have "tested" HWC, and trust me, indeed, it works in all markets. And that's because it is about price, price movement, and wave strength. And those are realities in any financial market. We accurately predicted the flash-crash years ago, and showed how it was a technical chart turning point, and had nothing to do with the SEC's determination of some computer glitch of some floor order. So yea, we are all about technical trading, not caring one bit about fundamentals (I can show you how they have no impact on price amplitudes, but it is true economic announcements can impact the timing of those price amplitudes ... typically accelerating the high and low of them). All that being said, if you are trading something other than Forex, while you will find our discoveries of price movement fascinating, I have not ported our technology to other platforms and markets for routine trading. But if you are, or want to be, a Forex trader, put your seat belts on, please!

Let's first understand that HWC is not the same as harmonic chart patterns (a la Gartley Patterns). HWC is based on a harmonic price movement and consistent strength exhaustion at the termination of a given time period's wave (or correction).

The power in HWC is that the primary measurement tool, the MultiWave indicator, can read up to seven (7) different time periods' wave strengths, and combine a plot of them onto any one chart of any given time period. It would take a trader viewing 5 to 7 charts to be able to analyze what MultiWave can do on one chart. Thus, I can view the precise time (typically within a 3-pip to 5-pip zone) of entry on my 1-minute chart, and without my eyes leaving that 1-minute chart, I can see EXACTLY what the 3-min, 5-min, 10-min, 30-min, 60-min, 240-min time period's waves are doing. It is the patterns generated by the plots of these multiple time period wave strengths that lead the way to analysis of when a particular price move is completed and ready for true reversal, just resting a bit before proceeding further, or entering a standard correction period. And I can tell that just moments after a wave hits its high or low point!

We are not measuring, nor is HWC, about Elliott Wave. However, HWC does use the understanding that is the premise within Elliott Wave, and that is, a longer term wave cannot terminate unless the lower level wave beneath it is also terminating (and the lower level wave below that lower level wave, and so on).

So what was truly the driving force to discover Harmonic Wave Convergence? It was pretty simple, actually. I was demo-trading in my typical, $50,000 demo-trading account, and getting excited, like most new traders, about the absolute dollars that could be made. I had terrible losses, as well. I knew nothing about position-sizing, and risk was just a word and concept. I soon realized that the big dollar gains I was being shown required the kind of capital that was in a demo account. But that if I were to scale my account down, use reasonable risk in the trade, that my earnings (again, with the systems and trading I was being shown and taught) were not going to replace my F500 income any day soon. And I could be patient, but I am just saying, there's not a lot of transparency in many of the folks selling trading strategies and models.

I figured if I was going to be a trader, attempting to replace a job as my source of income, I'd have first understood the reality of the math. And the math, well, really had little to do with the account size (at least in how things worked). Let me explain. I needed a way to understand the real profit in a trade, and how it was calculated ... and that led me to learn what 95% of most traders today still do not understand, and that is fixed-percentage risk management. So to be brief, here is a quick review...

You want to enter a trade, so the only thing your trading station is concerned with is how many lots you are going to put into the trade ... then you click BUY or SELL, right? So how do you know (not guess) how many lots to put into your trades? Well, if you want to capture the real benefit of the Forex, and that is leverage, you will want to take advantage of compounding. That means, you will not be putting the same number of lots in your trades every trade. So then, how many lots do you put in, using fixed-percentage risk?

Let's assume you have a $5000 mini account (value of 1 pip = $1.00). You are using a 25-pip stop-loss (more about this later). You want to put 5% risk into your trade.

So the math would look like:

[(Account Balance) X (Risk)] / [(Size of Stop Loss) X (Value of 1 pip)]

So let's substitute our numbers:

($5000) x (5%) / (25) x ($1.00) = 10 Lots

We can now determine that for 5% risk, we are talking about $250. And the value for 1 lot is $25.00. So if we are going to risk $250 in the trade across 25 $1.00 lots, we can put 10 lots into the trade. (review and review until you understand this completely).

In this example, we are saying, we are prepared for price to back up 25-pips before our trade would be terminated as having gone past our risk tolerance (established money management that you are comfortable with ... another completely different class/discussion). And if the price does go back that far, our trading station will take us out. And in this case, we'd lose $250 from our account balance.

From a "be transparent" standpoint, while I was taught 5% is acceptable risk, I can tell you it is not. For many reasons. First, you may not even be able to put 5% into a trade because of margin requirements with your broker / country. Secondly, even if you can, it's a terrible bet on the psychological side (again, another completely different class/discussion).

For newer traders, I never recommend more than 2% with live money, and the newest of the new should use no more than 1% (until they prove their consistency).

One quick note about risk. And that is, the math that generates lots in the trade based on risk and stop loss, also readily generates profit potential. This is what I meant about account balance not being necessary to project results. Here's what I mean ...

If you are risking 5% in your trade, using a 25-pip stop-loss, that means if you lose 25-pips, you've lost 5% of your account. However, on the flip-side, if you GAIN 25-pips, you gain 5% on your account. Don't get too excited, while 5% ROA (Return on Account) seems awesome, remember, a loss includes a 5% loss. And until you have your profit consistency, 5% losses will either burn out your trading account, or burn out your head. That's why it's way too high to play with as a trader!

So, I started playing with this math, and after reviewing dozens upon dozens of strategies and considerations, I quickly realized some simple realities. If I traded 2% using a 100-pip stop loss, it would take 100-pips of gain to get a 2% ROA. Likewise, if I traded 2% using a 10-pip stop-loss, it would take only 10-pips of gain to get a 2% ROA.

I quickly realized that there are many more 10-pip opportunities in a given trading time period than there are 100-pip opportunities. I quickly concluded that if I can gain 2% in 10-pips, that made a lot more sense than trying to gain 2% in 100-pips. That didn't mean I didn't want 100-pip trades, it just meant if I was going to entertain one, I'd enjoy making 10X the profit than the trader using the 100-pip stop-loss!

So it was easy for me, I saw the 100-pip opportunities that typically required the 100-pip stop-losses, and I started to look at where my trading capital was, and where I wanted It to be. If my gains were going to be with safe risk (2%), and I needed 100-pip trades to get 2%, it would take a long, long time to realize an account of any size. I quickly concluded, I needed a strategy that would let me precisely trade with a 10-pip stop-loss, and have a high percentage of wins, as well.

The problem was, I couldn't find one that fit that bill.

I don't have the space to detail just how I discovered Harmonic Wave Convergence, but it did have something to do with my frustration in understanding that the theory of Elliott Wave made sense to me, but my reality was not in being able to trade it for consistent profit.

The last thing I will say, is that most traders are led to believe that the smaller the stop-loss, the smaller the time frame you have to trade. Hence, when you move up in time-frames, you must have larger stop-losses. Well, this is true for most old-paradigm (the current way traders are taught). And that has to do with lagging indicators for the most part, and the reliance on them to enter and exit trades.

With HWC and the MultiWave Indicator, I can enter a 1-min, or a 4-hour trade, with a 10-pip or less stop-loss. Again, that means for every 10-pips gained, the account grows 2%. A simple and quick 10-pip trade, well, that's a 2% ROA. A trade that goes 60-pips, that's a 12% ROA. You can do your own math to project. And then, use your trading account size to project where your trading account may go. So the reality we have with HWC is it's ability to let us enter trades, with laser-like precision, and have minimum risks, with maximum yields.

For more information contact Steve Gregor

SteveGregor@PipClub.com

A Simple Edge for Active Traders by Eloy Fenocchi

I will be talking about exploiting opportunities created by crowd bias, which are my favorite type of trade setups, I will show you a simple trade setup today, some background information on it that I think you'll find interesting, and simple to trade. Remember there is risk in trading. Don't trade with money you can't afford to lose, and understand that there is no such thing as trades without risk.

Just a brief (overview) of my agenda: I'm going to be talking about cognitive biases, and why they're more robust. I'll give you brief examples of that, it makes perfect sense and although they're harder to come by, and harder to identify, observe and quantify, I think they're the best types of trades.

I'll show you why I have that belief. I'll show you a little about my statistics and studies, as it relates to this trading setup that I'm going to show you today. Then we'll go look at some stocks and how they relate to this strategy that I'm showing you; and then how you can employ the strategy yourself, using options for example - it's a very simple thing to do; and then how you can sign up for free alerts on our website www.marketsavvy.net Hopefully you'll find that instructional and helpful.

Here are some examples, and using a quote from "Way of the Turtle" by Curtis Faith, I quote: "...An exploitable statistical advantage based on market behavior that is likely to recur in the future, in trading, the best edges come from the market behaviors caused by cognitive biases." Now, that's kind of a big phrase 'cognitive bias', and unless you've thought about this, looked it up, or heard someone talk about it, it may not make sense to you right away, but a simple example is making reference to fear, or greed, in trading; we're making reference to a cognitive bias. Another way that we hear about cognitive biases would be "the crowd / herd mentality", if you can identify these emotional tendencies of human nature, which is another way of saying cognitive bias of human nature, then you're likely to find that's much more repeatable and that you can have confidence that it's likely to occur again, because people tend to do the same things at the same events or intervals, or when they are experiencing certain emotional urges. These things are more likely to be more robust in nature because they are human experience-related as opposed to the wholesale application of indicators on a chart.

So, another way of saying this is, and you might recognize the phrase, "buy the rumor, sell the news". How can you apply that? It's something that's been long recognized but not well understood, and how to apply it around certain events. So what I'll do is talk about earnings as the event, and I'll show you how I came to test these things to see if there's actually an advantage in doing it, and I'll show you the information that's needed to systematize this into a trading method.

So we're talking about specifically buying something, or a particular stock, and we like to use call options for example, or call option spreads, so we would buy these ahead of the earnings, and then we would sell these prior to the news, so we're buying the expectation of earnings, and then selling the news, that is, getting out of the way before the news is released. We expect markets to go up in anticipation of earnings, though they might continue to go up from there, but often a market will move up in anticipation of an event, and then will sell off after the event is known.

I'll also show you the specific rules on how you can do this. I'll show you my stock list, but before that I'd like to show you how I came across this and how I tested this, looking at my chart. What you're seeing is very simple; you'll notice that on the chart you have a long entry, "LE". We're simply saying that "x" number of days ahead of earnings we want to go long; and the blue line is an approximation of where earnings will be, it plots it in the future so you can see it's not exactly perfect but based on past data. It shows us where the earnings are likely to come in, it also gives us a price target, but I'm not concentrating on that. What I want to concentrate on is the advantage in buying the rumor and selling the news before earnings. This is not observable in all stocks, so I have a list of stocks that I'll go through, you can see my list of favorite stocks on my radar screen, but we can go through and quickly look at some of the numbers, so you can see the statistics behind something like this.

Adobe is 81%, so what this tells us is that 81% of the time, if we were to go long Adobe ahead of earnings by "x" number of days, 2-3 weeks, then we have a statistical advantage in doing that, and this is over a 5-year period of time. So, I'll go through and click on the different stocks so you can see. This one is 68%. Green Mountain Coffee: 56%. LinkedIn is almost 70%. Netflix: 70%. Google's a bit weak in this area, it's only about 50%, but it moves so much that we can usually get a trade out of this with no problem; It's one that I still like. AAPL: 70%. Do that about 20 days before earnings: buying the stock, and getting out a day or two before the earnings report. The system attempts to get us out the day before, and sometimes 2 days before. I'll go through a couple more. BIDU: 68%. MA: 70%. Visa: 76%. Amazon: 70%. Whole Foods: 65%. VMW: 62%. Chipotle Mexican, one of our favorites.

There are no short trades because the crowd is unlikely to be selling short stock number one, most people don't: (a) know how to do it, and (b) they think only in terms of being long the market, so it's not the same thing.

EMC: 76%. Red Hat: 75%. Boeing: 75%. Caterpillar...

I could go on, but this is basically the top of my list. I wanted to show you statistically why I look at this particular method as an advantageous method. Average best day prior to earnings for entry, this is 17 days, I showed this as an example on our September 15th seminar in Dallas with TradeStation, and I gave this particular one as a trade example, which is Chipotle Mexican. The day that it went long was on the 24th, on the 15th (a Sunday) which was the day of the seminar, the closest one that I had was Chipotle, so I gave that particular class that particular example. I'll show how I showed that to them, and the earnings should be either today or tomorrow. I want to show you the specific criteria on how you can do this simply without having to have anything but some simple tools, so you can use my special stock list I just gave you. I'm going to show you how to look for a chart pattern, I call it "the dip"; it's a dip chart pattern 2-3 weeks ahead of earnings. I'll show you a simple method that you can use.

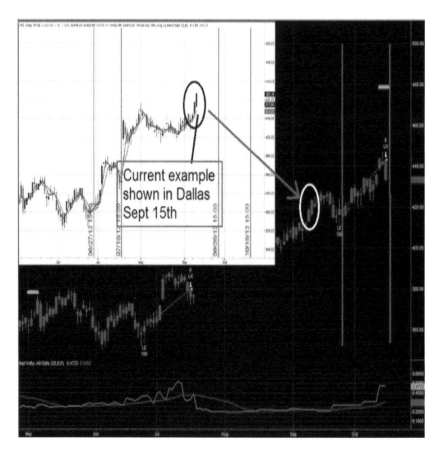

A manual method, but it's very simple and easy to do. You can look for a dip 2-3 weeks prior to earnings and a break-out pattern, I'll show you a couple of indicators you can use for that, simple moving averages, and then we're looking to buy up to a 30-day call option or a spread. You can choose whichever you want. If you're not used to doing spreads be careful because if you do spreads ahead of earnings and the strikes are too tight, then you're liable to be right and not make any money because implied volatility will be rising and that will potentially hurt your trade with the short option ballooning against you. The simplest thing to do is: look at an "at the money" (or one-two strikes out of the money) call option. You can use weeklies if you want, 2-3 weeks out, up to 30 days. It's simple. I don't use stops, I size the trade according to my risk tolerance, but I don't let the trade go to zero either. If the stock doesn't start to move in the expected direction in a few days I'll look to take it off.

Now, let me show you the chart pattern, and this is actually the example that I used in the class; here's specifically what I do: I go and find the earnings date, then I put a line to mark the date. So I found that on Chipotle, it was going to report earnings on the 18th of October. So in this case, this would be in July, so the Earnings is scheduled for July the 18th, so I'm going to put a vertical line on the chart to mark when the scheduled event is. In many cases you can actually set up an alert for that event. And then you go and on your chart just put a line 2-3 weeks before the scheduled event, and if you see a meaningful dip, as you can see here there's 3 or 4 days, 5 days, where the market went down in this case Google, went down right into that red line. Am I buying there? Well, yes I could, but I'm giving you something to help you to decide when to buy here, let's just put a 3 and a 5 period moving average and when that crosses over, then you want to go long, it's just an easy way for me to be able to show you - a line in the sand for you to be able to get in. It's pretty scary if the market's going down for you to get long here, so most people won't pull the trigger and they'll miss the trade anyway, so by using the 3 and 5 period moving average cross-over at least we're buying when the market's already turned around and going up. So it's simple and it feels right. You just take the stocks that I gave you, and you go create charts like this. Very simple, put a line on there when the event is going to be, when the earnings reports are going to be, and I'll show you in a minute how to find it. And then go out 2-3 weeks prior, you don't have to be exact about this, three days before, 3 days later, it's just we want to be in that neighborhood, 20 trading days out to earnings, that's generally when these things tend to be the best time to pick them up.

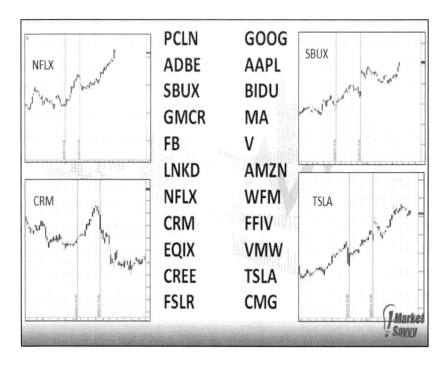

So my next chart shows you a couple of pictures, with examples of this. So here's Netflix, again I drew the line ahead of time, this is before the market I tend to adjust my trades when they're up 40-50%, because it gives me the ability to take money off the table and take that capital and play multiple plays with the same capital, and, if I'm wrong, I've already reduced the risk on the trade - it's a little more of an advanced type of discussion that we use and we have rules for all those things, but just to give you a little bit more flavor as to some of the kinds of things that you can think about doing. But the simple rules are: (a) you put the line on the chart when the earnings are going to be released, (b) you put a line 2-3 weeks ahead of that, (c) look for the dip in the stock, and (c) when you see your 3 and 5 moving average crossing over, (d) there's your trigger to get long.

You can easily find the earnings date for these from Bloomberg or Yahoo Finance. I hope the session was helpful.

For more information please visit www.marketsavvy.net and www.savvyfx.com

You can also reach Eloy directly via email: systems@marketsavvy.net

Trend Following Trades Addresses The Trend Traders Challenge of Trading Only Trending Markets with its Patent Pending TFT AMA by John Karnas

Here at Trend Following Trades, we have been trading a very visually simplistic Trend Following Method with great success. Our visually simplistic Method allows for Traders to make trading decisions based on an Indicator and Rule Set that doesn't "clutter up" the chart with many indicators that have to come into alignment in order to take high probability Trend Following Trades. The TFT Method works the same EXACT way regardless if you're intra-day, swing or position trading of Futures, Forex, Stocks, ETF's or Options on them.

Although many other "complicated" Methods may have decent individual performance, often trades are missed because of having to look at so much information, real-time, which leads to "decision lock", causing traders to miss good, valid trades as well as feeling like they have to take lower probability trades, late in the swing move. Also, not to mention what it would take (from a screen real-estate standpoint) to monitor and trade MANY markets!

We've now taken the VERY robust, back testable TFT Method, with great results, and brought it onto a "Grid" type of trading Platform that integrates seamlessly with NinjaTrader7. This is called the Trend Following Trades Advanced Market Administrator (TFT AMA). This product is just going into Beta Testing with a few existing members of TFT.

We have filters that keep us out of Non-Trending Markets, and now we no longer need to wait for the few markets that we may have been monitoring with individual charts, to begin trending or try and force trades that don't have the highest probability of success in the few markets that we used to look at. You can now trade up to 12 markets all on one monitor! In the future, Traders will be able to have multiple AMA's running, only restricting the number and time frames of markets that can be traded at once, by computer hardware limitations.

The TFT AMA is FAR more than just a Market Analyzer, it is a complete Market Administrator. It has many Market Analyzer functionalities, but also incorporates single click trade execution (with automatic price calculation of entry BEFORE the trade triggers) and money management functionality, according to the TFT Enhanced Chart Method and its Set-ups and trades. Along with this, is the ability to EASILY identify early trend indication, Short-Medium and Long Term market structure and conditions of divergence, ALL with a visually simplistic and easy to understand coloring cells in the TFT AMA, either Green for Bullish or Red for Bearish conditions (also light Green and Red for early notifications of these conditions).

The TFT AMA is designed to be used on half of a 1080P monitor, of any size, which will allow you to have charts up along side of the AMA for traditional Chart viewing of the TFT Standard Enhanced Chart method OR some other charts and other indicators that traders may feel valuable placed on any chart. Left side support and resistance identification of the market being traded can also be picked up looking at these charts. The TFT AMA can also be maximized on one monitor and charts can be pulled up on a second, third, etc. monitors, if desired.

Best Trading Strategies

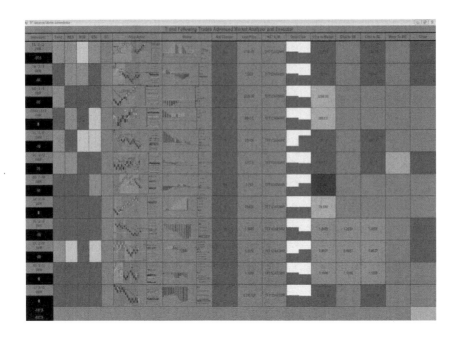

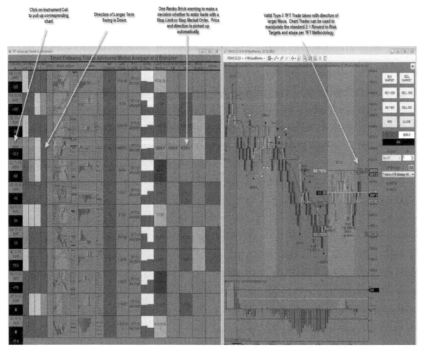

Once placed next to charts, you can click on the far left hand side cell of the TFT AMA (the one that shows the market and time frame) and the chart or charts of that market will immediately appear on the other side of the screen. If you are using NinjaTrader's Chart Trader, then all orders, stops and targets can be shown, manipulated there, AND/OR on a DOM that is located on another monitor. There is no longer the need for multiple time frame charts as the Market Structure cells (Middle and Long term) will show the longer term picture of Market Structure, that is often used as a filter to only take trades in the direction of the larger trend, on secondary, longer time frame charts.

Once an order is placed, the TFT AMA will automatically use a pre-selected NinjaTrader 7 ATM, cancel and resubmit the Stop Market or Stop Limit orders to a better price, if not triggered in on the current bar, the TFT AMA will give you the ability for a better price entry. Once that order is automatically re-submitted and the market continues to move away from the intended direction of the trade trigger, without triggering in, then the order will automatically be cancelled for good, for that particular set-up. Essentially making the TFT AMA a manual Auto Trader of the TFT Enhanced Chart Method! If there is no set-up warning on the AMA, then there is NO chance of taking a non-Method or non-planned trade, unless you decide to Market in by left clicking on the Market Order Cell OR right clicking on it for entry into the market, in the opposite direction (for those that chose to counter trend trade from the TFT AMA).

Best Trading Strategies

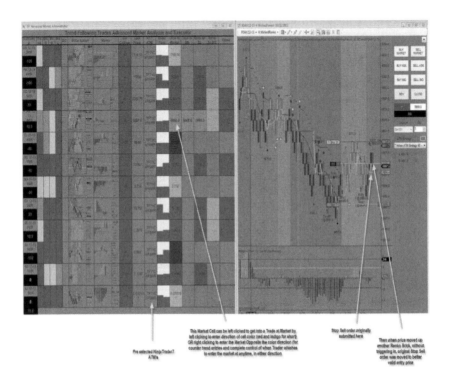

The most unique items of the TFT AMA are the Price Action and Momo Cells. These cells show a real-time condensed area of Panel 1 price and Panel 2 TFT Momo area of the Chart (there is an input for choosing the number of past bars you chose to see). This enables you to actually see real-time, Price movement and the TFT Momo indicator (and whatever else you have in Panel 1 and Panel 2) without ever having to pull up or look at a chart. This technology works for charts that aren't even being displayed on ANY monitor. This functionality allows Traders to see what's happening in up to 12 markets on Panel 1 and Panel 2 of a chart without having to have

ANY charts being displayed!

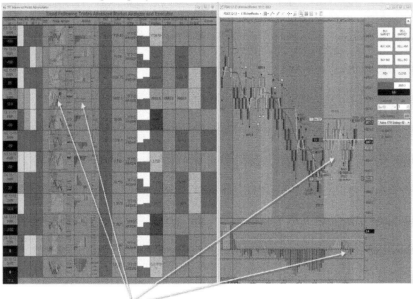

Notice how actual price area (Panel 1) and TFT Momo (Panel 2) as well as whatever else in on the chart, is displayed in these cells. This enables Traders to have a "chart peek" without having to actually pull up any chart.

The TFT AMA also has individual market close and move to Break Even cells. If a trade is in profit and at a point that you wish to remove the risk out of the trade, simply click on the Orange Break Even cell and the stop will automatically be moved to Break Even. If at ANYTIME you wish to exit the entire position, simply click on the close cell of the market that the position is in, and it will exit the position immediately (whether it's in profit or loss).

These functionalities are designed to be used to override any NinjaTrader 7 ATM's that are assigned and being used in any particular trade (i.e. if a double top, double bottom, area of support or resistance is being approached, before your first target, you can easily make in trade exit or money management decisions, right in the TFT AMA)!

Best Trading Strategies

Also displayed in the far left, Market Type and Time Frame cell, is the open and closed profit and loss for that trading session (very similar to what Ninjatrader 7 displays). The last row displays Global profit and loss, showing real-time open and closed profit and loss. If at any time you are in single or multiple positions and you decide that you want to exit ALL positions, the Global lower right hand close cell can be clicked on to immediately exit out of all positions (i.e. if you are at your daily target or stop loss, you can use this cell to go flat and be done trading).

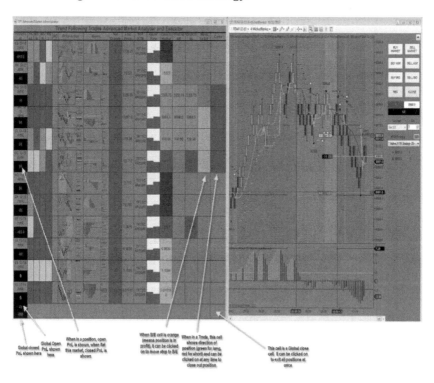

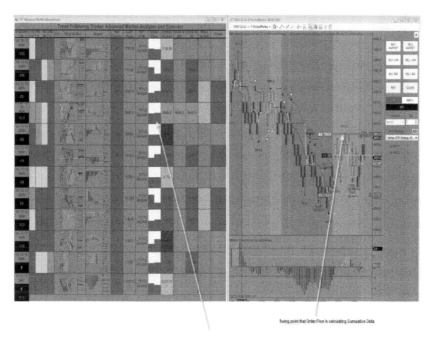

"Order Flow" cell. Notice that we enter this trade with "Net" Bis/Ask Accumulation, from last swing point is Net negative. This adds extra confirmation that Cumulative Delta of this Swing is still Net short when we enter our trade.

We have also added an Order Flow cell to the TFT AMA. This cell shows a percentage ratio between contracts that are being executed at the bid versus the ask, back to the last swing point of your choice (short, middle or long). This type of "Cumulative Delta" Swing Order Flow, helps traders to determine whether a pullback into the TFT "Value Area" is simply profit taking OR if Traders are actually initiating larger positions opposite to the current swing (i.e If looking to go short, you may want to make sure that the Red bar on the Order Flow cell is higher than the Green bar). This simple yet powerful tool addresses what we consider to be the last form of volume that still has trading decision validity. The massive amount of High Frequency Trading Volume or "Black Box" Algorithms have really disrupted the reading of standard up and down volume of each price bar, so now we're looking at the most recent Swing.

Next I'd like to discuss the robustness of any Method or Trading System. If you can define rules that can be programmed for Auto Trading, why wouldn't you do it? Well, the answer is real simple. Many Systems out there work well only during very short times of the day or under VERY restrictive market conditions.

We are so confident in our Method/System performance that our returning Trade Room will be running Auto Trading Strategies, with real money, based off of the same exact rules that are taught for discretionary trading. Entries and Exits will be shown in real-time for all to see (no deceiving Trade Room games). We are doing this so that we can discuss and educate on specific trade set-ups real-time, without worry about missing or miss managing OUR trades. Instead of concentrating on our own trading and leaving members to have to wait until our daily stops or targets are achieved, we will be talking about Trades as they set-up and execute automatically.

We believe that we will be the first organization in the World that will be doing this!

The TFT Enhanced Method Auto Trader will be offered for sale to all Lifetime license holders of the TFT AMA. We will also have a TFT AMA Auto Trader that will have the capability (based on account risk restrictions) to take positions in multiple markets, simultaneously. We will monitor, restrict and charge a small fee for the number of contracts that these Auto Traders take in the live market at any given price at the same exact point in time. It is VERY important to put the restriction of number of contracts entered and exited at the same price and time, in order to keep the performance of ANY Auto Trader consistent with its past performance (even though past performance doesn't guarantee future performance).

Different markets will have different restrictions based on the size of the Bid and Ask being offered, as well as, the overall volume in any particular market (i.e. The Mini S&P and Bonds will be restricted to around 500 contracts, while markets like Gold and Crude Oil will be restricted to around 25 contracts). These are initial numbers and if we find that these adversely affect the Auto Trading performance, they will be adjusted to the downside, conversely, if we find that performance isn't effected, they'll be adjusted to the upside until performance is effected, essentially looking for a point of balance where what we do doesn't affect "normal" market movement and price fills.

Please look for these Auto Traders to be released for sale/lease in the beginning of next year (2014), along with co-location hardware packages.

Of late, high frequency trading (HFT) and Algorithmic (Black Box) has taken over most of the trading volume in the markets today. Therefore, standard volume indicators that worked in the past are becoming less and less reliable moving forward. One thing that has not changed though (through our own extensive historical back testing), is price action using certain types of Renko Bars. Although the markets have become a lot "choppier" because of HFT and Black Box trading, the price patterns, price bars and the TFT Method that we use, still remains intact. Recognizing and reacting to these price patterns has been my key to success, as well as, NOT having to be right 80% of the time to make decent money, when trading less than a targeted 2:1 Reward to risk ratio.

What is very interesting is that certain Trend Trading price patterns show up in almost all types of time frames that are traded. In the case of "Outside-In" or Countertrend Trading of areas of "Confluence" and other areas, these price patterns are less clear and traders rely more on "areas" that they feel price will turn around.

They often take VERY small profits (less than 10 ticks) and encourage adding "size" to make more money. We believe in trying to capture as much of the swing as possible, with every position traded (and taking partial profits along the way), as the key to long term sustainable success.

Since tradable volume patterns can no longer simply be identified at these areas, because of HFT and Black Box trading, moving forward traders will find themselves having even more of a difficult time successfully trading "Outside-In" methods. Many companies are creating tools to help identify HFT activity; however, HFT activity by its very nature can go either way. So as Trend Following Traders, we actually like HFT activity, because it shows us that volume is active in the market and knowing that "Early" trends tend to continue (at least one more push or wave 3 for Elliot Wave Traders) before they reverse (unless they are at obvious areas of left side price support or resistance). Most of the time this helps ensure our success to greater than a 50% win to loss ratio. At a 2:1 targeted win loss ratio (which is what our method promotes and is based on) we will make decent money, with far less stress in trading at the 50% win/loss ratio. As Traders become more proficient with the TFT Method or use TFT Automated Strategies, long term win loss ratios at 2:1 can exceed 70%.

The existence of new bar types such as, Wicked Renko and other Renko bars, remove a lot of this HFT "noise" and helps us to identify the true movement of the swing. No volume, number of trades, or time components exist in these bars, which allows price pattern recognition along with price momentum reading to not be effected by HFT or Black Box Trading "noise".

If you have any further interest in finding out about what is discussed above, please do not hesitate to contact us at info@trendfollowingtrades.com and/or visiting us at www.trendfollowingtrades.com (a new website will be launched before the end of 2013). You can also subscribe or follow us on YouTube, Twitter, and Facebook, where we will be once again posting trading videos with entry and exit markers to show our successes and failures in trading. We have been keeping a VERY low profile until waiting for the completion of TFT AMA. Now that it's about to go into Beta, we will become more active in promoting the Company, products and our Mission Statement - to become the last stop on a Traders journey to consistent profitability.

You can find us by our name, Trend Following Trades, in most of these areas of social media.

John Karnas

Owner/Trader/Educator

www.TrendFollowingTrades.com

USE THIS 4-STEP TRADING PROCESS OR YOU MAY FIND YOURSELF IN A 12-STEP PROGRAM BY JOHN MATTESON

You have probably heard over and over again that before you start trading, you need a plan. This is absolutely true. What gets lost too often, however, is the phase or bridge between your trading plan and your actual trade setup and execution. This bridge is absolutely necessary for success in trading. All of the successful traders I know or have read about always cross this bridge before taking a single trade in their trading plan. I refer to this bridge in many of my presentations as the 4-Step Trading Process. If you don't have a bridge or process in place currently, then you are welcome to adopt this one. If you do have a process you currently use, it may be worded a bit differently but should cover these same bases. As you will see, these 4 steps will allow you to obey the golden rule of trading – cut your losses short and let your winners run.

Step 1. Find a trade

This one should be pretty obvious. You have to have a trade promise, setup or setups in order to enter the market to the long or short side. These setups should be part of your trading plan but you have to be able to recognize them in a live situation without hesitation.

Step 2. Assess the risk to reward

Just because you have uncovered a trade setup doesn't necessarily mean you should take it. First, you need to determine if the reward side of the equation is worth taking on the initial risk. I recommend you only take trades where the reward side of the trade equation is at least twice the size of the initial risk. For example, let's say I have

$20,000 of risk capital and you only risk 1% of that $20k on any 1 trade. This means the maximum risk, in terms of dollars, will be $200 on any given trade. If you are going to risk $200 on a trade, then you want to see a potential reward of at least $400 or two times your initial risk at your initial target to consider taking the trade. If the reward is anything less than twice your initial maximum risk, then you should pass on the trade and look for something elsewhere that has a better risk to reward proposition.

This is a very important part of the process that you cannot skip if you want to have long-term success. Why? The majority of failing traders have small wins and big losses. This means they may be winning 80% of their trades but they still end up losing money. If there is one thing you can change about your trading, this is it: take small risks and have larger rewards. Do the opposite of what 90% of those losing money do. Some very skillful traders can make a 1 to 1 risk/reward proposition work over time, but they are the exception rather than the rule.

There are several reasons why using a reward side of the equation that is at least twice the size of the initial risk is better. One is simple human error. You are going to make mistakes in your trading. Hitting the sell button when you meant to buy, trading the wrong size position accidentally, etc. If you require a high percentage of winners, one mistake can mean the difference between being profitable or not at the end of the month. Another reason why you should consider taking larger rewards is that sometimes technology will fail. You might lose power in your home or trading office, your internet connection may fail, your trading platform malfunctions or there is a flash crash or a piece of news comes out that moves the market. These are things that are out of your control and will happen to you if you trade long enough. If you are taking small wins, even 1 times your initial risk, a big loss that is out of your control can really damage your account. It may take a while to dig out of a hole like this if you take small wins even if you normally take small losses.

If, on the other hand, your wins are typically at least twice the size of your initial risk and you run into one of these disasters which produce a loss that is, say, 5 times the size of your normal risk, you may be able to make this loss back in 1 good trade. If you take rewards that are only 1 time your initial risk or less, and you lose 5 times your initial risk due to disaster, you will need 5 wins in order to make up for 1 loss. Assess your risk to reward before each trade and make sure your potential reward is at least twice the size of your initial risk. If it isn't, then pass.

Chart 1. shows a natural gas trade setup taken by one of our clients. You can see he has followed the 4-step trading process and has found a trade setup, assessed the risk to reward, determined the correct position size based on his risk tolerance, capital and size of the stop required.

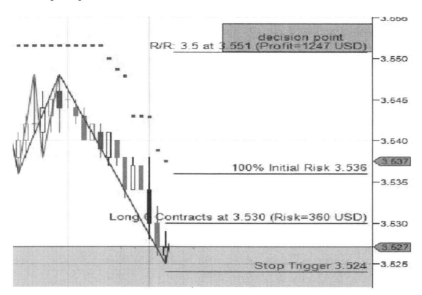

Chart 1.

Chart 2 shows the result of the NG trade. Even though the trader had a proper stop in place for what would normally be a 1R loss (1 risk unit or $360), disaster struck when the NG price dropped suddenly and turned what should have been a small $360 loss into a 5R loss of $1800. These disasters will happen during your trading career. The best way to recover from unplanned, large losses is to take big wins. If you typically take small wins, you may never be able to dig out of these disasters. Taking small, controlled risks along with larger rewards will hold you in good stead over the long term.

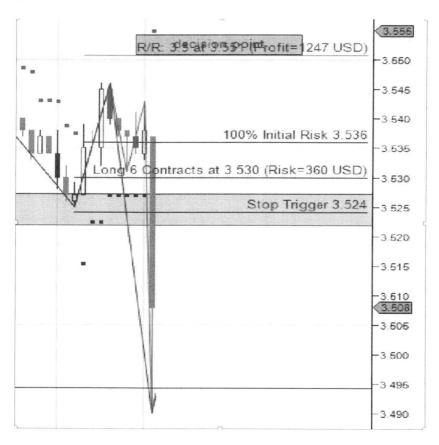

Chart 2.

Step 3. Determine your correct position size

This is one aspect of trading that many traders have either forgotten or never learned. The goal here is to keep your risk profile consistent from trade to trade, market to market and time frame to time frame. So, whether you are trading from a daily chart of the Euro or a 3 minute chart of the S&P, the dollar amount you have at risk will be the same. This way, when you lose, you lose consistently small.

For example, let's say you are trading with $20,000 of risk capital and the maximum you are going to risk on any one trade is 1% or $200. This means you have $200 to risk, regardless of the market or time frame (tick, range, Renko etc.) you are trading from. What will change is the number of shares, contracts or lots you can trade based on the size of the stop that is required. Let's say you are trading from a 3 minute chart of the Dow mini. You have found a trade and have determined the reward is $600 or 3 times your initial risk of $200. The stop required is 10 points from your entry. Since each point in the YM is worth $5/contract, this means your $200 maximum risk will allow you to trade 4 contracts ($200 max risk/10 point stop/$5 = 4 contracts).

Now, let's say your next trade is from the 15 minute chart of the YM. The stop required for this trade is 20 points from the entry. Again, since each point in the YM is worth $5, your $200 risk limit will now only allow you to purchase 2 contracts ($200/20pt stop/$5 = 2 contracts). Even though you can trade more contracts on the smaller time frame and fewer contracts on the larger time frame, the dollar amount at risk has not changed in either case. This will keep any losses consistently small and will help you obey the "cut losses short" part of the golden rule.

Chart 3 shows the same trader who lost 5R on the NG trade earlier in the day due to a circumstance out of his control, come back with this ES 3 minute trade setup. Once again he follows the 4-step trading process and takes a small controlled risk with a position size based on the size of his risk capital and his risk tolerance. He has chosen a market based target that is 7 times his initial risk. You can see he has his entry, stop, correct position size and initial target defined before he executes the trade.

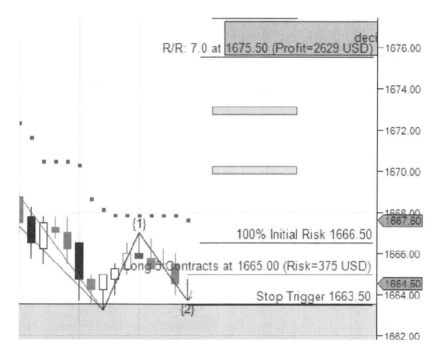

Chart 3

Step 4. Control your exit strategy in order to maximize profits

For every trade, you should have your entry, stop, correct position size and initial target planned before you enter the market. Once you are in a trade and the trade begins to play out as anticipated, you need a way to determine whether you should be sticking with

Best Trading Strategies

your initial target as planned or if you should perhaps be trailing the price with a trailing stop or some other stop placement strategy to potentially capture more profit in the direction of your trade.

The MTPredictor software has a strength band indicator built into its Strong Trend Filter which gives the trader an indication of potential strength in the direction of a trade. This allows the trader to make a decision on whether to pass on their initial target and instead trail with an ATR trailing stop in an effort to capture more profit. This last step also helps the trader to obey the "let the winners run" part of the golden rule.

Chart 4 shows the result of the ES trade that our MTPredictor client took. After losing $1800 (-5R) on his first trade, he came back with this $2629 win. The net result of continuing to follow the 4 step-trading process was a profit of $829 (2R+). This also shows the power of taking small losses and having bigger wins. Even when disaster strikes, you can come back with one good trade and recover the loss and even add to your profit total!

Chart 4

Speakers of Traders World Online Expo #14

Remember, the process is simple but It will make a huge impact on your trading when you couple it with a solid trading plan. Let's review the process here:

Find a trade

Assess the risk to reward

Determine your correct position size

Control your exit strategy in order to maximize profits

Use this process before every trade you take and you might just save yourself from ending up in a 12 step program. :-)

For more information contact John Matteson www.mtpredictor.us

THE GARTLEY TRADING METHOD BY ROSS BECK

Figure 27

The original Gartley Pattern (shown above) has a very different look and feel compared to how it is being taught today. The original Gartley Pattern was quite a simple pattern. Gartley did not discuss any Fibonacci ratios, Elliott Wave, etc. In Gartley's bullish example, it would appear that all he is looking for is a significant rally off of a bottom, followed by a retracement of 33% to 50%.

Based on Gartley's example, the original pattern only included four data points or three legs. It is of interest that the modern version of the Gartley Pattern does not include Gartley's A-B leg. In Elliott Wave terms, the original pattern would appear to be the completion of a Wave Two. That means that if the pattern works, you would be trading a Wave three, a trade that most Elliotticians would consider very difficult to identify.

If you search the internet for information about the Gartley pattern, you will find the description of a complex five point pattern that has to conform to specific Fibonacci ratios on each of it's four legs.

The main differences between the modern Gartley Pattern above and the original Gartley Pattern are...

1. The labels in the original pattern are A,B,C. The labels for the modern pattern are X,A,B,C,D.

2. The modern Gartley omits the original A-B leg.

3. The modern Gartley emphasizes the equality of the A-B leg and the C-D leg whereas the original does not.

4. The original Gartley pattern did not include any Fibonacci ratios.

5. The completion of the original pattern was at 33%-50% whereas the modern pattern completes at the 78.6% retracement of the XA move.

Larry Pesavento was the first person to apply Fibonacci ratio's to the Gartley pattern. Larry observed that the Gartley pattern appeared to be a more reliable pattern if it completed at a 61.8% retracement or 78.6% retracement. Based on my 10+ years of experience with the Gartley pattern, it appears that if you have to choose between the two of these ratios, 78.6% seems to work the best. With my personal trading, I will only trade the 78.6% Gartley patterns. Why? I would rather trade less often and increase the chances of my wins on the few trades that I make. If you feel a need to trade more often, it may be time to take a personal inventory. We need patience to wait for good Gartley Patterns, remember Gartley himself said, "The art in conducting an operation of this kind lies in.. having the patience to wait …".

In addition, one of the added benefits of using the 78.6% retracement is its proximity to where our protective stop is located. Remember Gartley said," In the other two cases, only small losses have to be taken". So if we choose the 78.6% versus the 61.8% Fibonacci level to enter, our risk will be reduced if we use the location Gartley suggested for our stop. If we are wrong, we will risk less money with an entry at 78.6% versus 61.8%.

One of the other reasons that I prefer the 78.6% level is that the public is typically unaware of this level as it does not appear in the defaults of most Fibonacci retracement drawing tools. Therefore there is contrarian value in using this level. Also, by the time a market arrives at 78.6%, most of the typical 61.8% fib traders have been stopped out. At this point in time, there is a lot of uncertainty as traders watch for a bounce or a break based on their focus on the previous high or low. Also, typically there is an increase in the volatility in the 78.6% retracement area as the market begins to reflect the uncertainty of its participants. The volatility in this zone will help us if we enter with a multiple contract strategy that allows us to leverage the scale out of the market.

For more information, read The Gartley Trading Method: New Techniques to Profit From the Market's Most Powerful Formation on Amazon.

Contact Ross Beck, FCSI CEO, Geometric Trading LLC

www.GeometricTrading.com

The Mystery of Interest Rate Futures and the Stars by Barry William Rosen

Most Gann aficionados know that Gann used astrology and that the most successful traders use in their trading as it is the hidden undercurrent that runs the markets. J.P. Morgan, the founder of the Morgan bank, was fond of saying that "anyone can be a millionaire, but to become a billionaire, you need an astrologer." He had a private astrologer, Evageline Adams, who helped him tremendously. I have been fortunate to purchase financial astrological books from her library.

It is a little known fact that W. D. Gann went to India and studied Indian Sidereal Astrology. In his notebooks we find sketches of astrological symbols on his charts; and in his memoirs, he discusses his journey to India. In fact, the famous Gann wheel was first used by tea merchants in seventeenth century India. Interest rate futures can be successfully traded by understanding planetary aspects and movements. This article will attempt to suggest trading techniques combining heliocentric astrology, sidereal or Indian astrology, and traditional technical analysis to improve your interest rate futures trading score.

THE PLANETS AND THE INTEREST RATE FUTURES

So what are the most important planets according to Sidereal astrology? Mars, which governs debt, would have to be the most important signifier; Pluto, which is its higher octave, would have to be of equal importance. Mercury, which is the ascendant lord of Virgo, of the 1977 natal futures chart is of secondary importance. And the Sun, which governs government, has to be of great significance also.

Geocentric aspects appear more important than heliocentric aspects in pinpointing swing turns. Aspects to the Sun are always significant, with Mercury conjunctions a great surge of energy and movement; trines from Neptune and Jupiter also appear to create important and bold movements.

Sextiles from Saturn and oppositions and major squares by Saturn also have an important effect which is usually bearish, as it suggests more tightening by the government.

Trines and conjunctions from Uranus are usually friendly but may create some surprise during government report.

Major aspects to Pluto are always significant, and since they do not occur that often they should be watched carefully. Pluto's stationary and retrograde activity twice a year often create major energy for bigger movements. Major aspects to Mars should also be watched closely. Conjunctions and squares with Mercury are usually not that friendly for the market, nor are aspects from Saturn. Aspects with Venus, especially conjunctions with Venus, are extremely energetic; aspects with Neptune are also highly energetic and speculative; aspects with Uranus are usually wild and unpredictable. Mars and Pluto aspects are usually negative for the T-Bond market.

We have outlined some of the important aspects, but because there are so many planets involved with Interest rate futures and their interactions, we would watch Mars, Mercury, Pluto and the Sun and the major planets and their exact aspects.

The stationary/ retrograde and stationary/direct movements of the following planets create a great deal of energy in the Interest rate futures market, and may lead to acceleration of a move and provide major swing turn points: Mercury, Pluto,

Neptune, Uranus and Mars seem to have the most impact on the market. Mercury and Pluto stations occur more often than Mars stations.

SUMMARY

We take the above information and chart it on a sidereal calendar and note pockets of strength and weakness and then combine it with traditional technical tools. We particularly like Elliott Wave and stochastics and Fibonacci retracement numbers as being the most useful. In addition to your technical arsenal of trendlines, Gann Squares, Elliott Wave counts, stochastics, RSI, etc., use the following planetary information for entering and exiting T-Bond trades at key support and resistance levels. In using the information below, keep the market's context and major trend in mind by examining monthly and weekly charts. The influences below will not be as strong in a bull market as it is in a bear market.

Note the following on your calendar:

I. a) Circle the major aspects, (i.e. conjunctions, squares, trines and sextiles as outlined above; looking at geocentric aspects of Mars, Pluto, Mercury and the Sun, and also note the stationary/retrograde movements noted above. Note: Indian astrology does not consider sextile aspects except between Saturn and other planets to be important. Trines and squares between certain planets are less important and are not considered full aspects. (See references below for additional information on sidereal aspects).

b) Do the same for HELIOCENTRIC ASPECTS; however, give them secondary significance. Geocentric aspects between Pluto, Mars and the other planets may be more important turns than minor aspects between Mercury and the outer planets, which occur more often.

c) Note important transits of Mars, Mercury, Pluto and the Sun as well as important stationary and retrograde movements.

bearish.

Ill. Combine astrology with technicals. Consider:

1) What is the major trend on the weekly chart? The daily chart? The 60-minute chart? Examine stochastics. Try to line up all three to trade in the direction of the trend or at least the daily and 60-minute charts should line up.

2) Examine Elliott wave patterns. Is the market oversold and completing a minor or major pattern as we come into a minor or major aspect? When geocentric or heliocentric aspects occur overnight, expect a change of trend in the night session or within the first 15 minutes of trading. If oversold conditions exist and the trend is higher and the aspects and energy turn bullish, then you have a major buying situation setting up.

3) Since the T-bond market's price structure responds especially well to Fibonacci retracements and projections, use ratios of .382,.500 and .618 and .782 and 1.618 to help determine price.

4) Use other technical tools such as Elliott Wave, Andrews Lines or Gann to give you additional information.

Space permits a case study or future prediction for the T-note market but those are available on my website at www.fortucast.com Email support@fortucast.com

Speakers of Traders World Online Expo #14

Slope and Noise – Relationship to Profit by Brady Preston

Martingale and anti-martingale betting systems have both been used to improve equity curves. The martingale betting system doubles the bet after every loss, so the first win could cover all previous losses. Traders recognize the problem with this because the bet size could reach such a large size that the bet size would be larger than the remaining capital. With this problem known traders instead of doubling their betting size will add to their bet while in a losing streak. Anti-martingale is the opposite of this and the trader is looking to add to the bet size while they are on a winning streak. These types of betting systems are also very similar to trend following and mean reversion systems. Martingale is very similar to mean reversion because in mean reversion the trader is buying market weakness. Anti-martingale is similar to trend following because the trader is buying market strength. An interesting point that I have discovered is that an anti-martingale generally won't improve the results from trend following systems. In this article I would like to cover some of the reasons why I believe this is true.

Below you will see an equity curve from a simple trend following system. I have also added a moving average to this equity to demonstrate how effective the moving average would be at filtering the equity curve. As you can see the equity curve continually bounces back and forth over the equity curve.

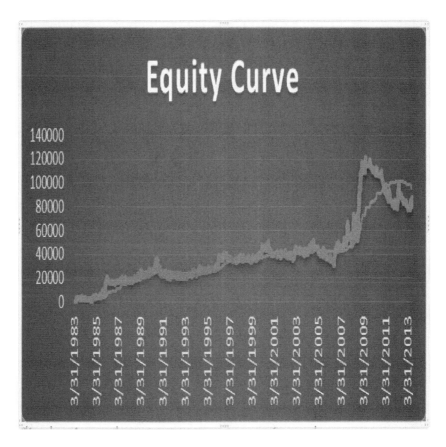

This is why anti martingale under performances when applied to trend following systems. If you were to buy into new highs the equity curve would quickly turn back down. I believe the main reason why this approach works or not has to do with the relationship between slope and noise.

The easiest way to see the slope of an equity curve is to add a trendline. Below you will see that I have now added a trendline to the chart with the equity curve. With the trendline added to the chart it is very easy to calculate the slope of the trendline.

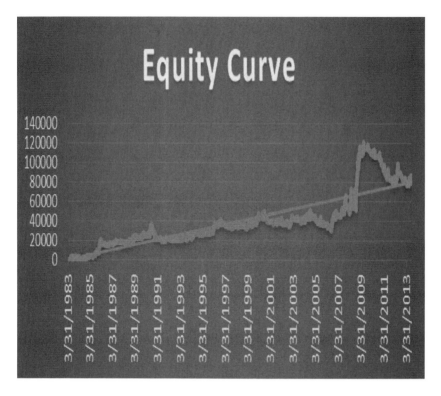

The slope of the trendline is calculated by dividing the difference of the y-coordinates of a point on the trendline by the difference of the x-coordinates. Once we know the slope of the trendline any point can be constructed by using the following formula Y = mx + b. The formula is fairly easy to understand.

Y = the Y value of the point

m = the slope of the trendline

x = the X value of the point

b = the y value where the trendline intercepts the y axis

The formula can be taken one step further by adding a noise value to the formula. This will allow us to not only construct the trendline, but also the equity curve. With the noise element added to the formula is looks like this:

Y = mx + b + e

On the chart below you will see the full formula for our equity curve. The formula below is to calculate the noise at each x value. The noise value is the difference between the trendline and the actual equity point. We will need to calculate and store a noise value for each x value so that it can be used later to reconstruct the equity curve.

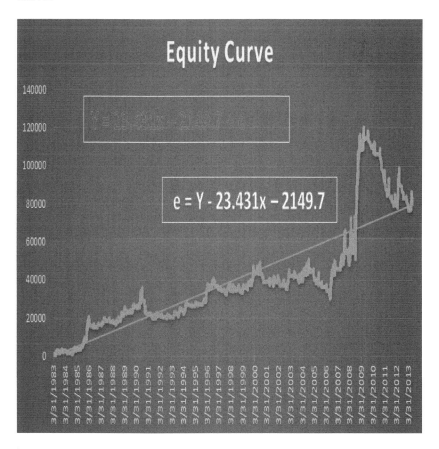

The table below shows the results of calculating first the noise for each point on the equity curve and then using the noise to reconstruct the equity curve. The noise column was constructed by subtracting the trendline from the equity. The advantage of being able to reconstruct the equity line with the formula is that we can isolate the noise and slope levels. Once we have the slope and noise levels isolated we can then individually adjust these levels to see how it affects the betting systems performance.

Period	Equity	Trendline	Noise	Calculated
0.00	-110	-2149.7	2039.7	-110
1.00	40	-2126.27	2166.269	40
2.00	310	-2102.84	2412.838	310
3.00	500	-2079.41	2579.407	500
4.00	770	-2055.98	2825.976	770
5.00	980	-2032.55	3012.545	980
6.00	860	-2009.11	2869.114	860
7.00	1430	-1985.68	3415.683	1430
8.00	1420	-1962.25	3382.252	1420
9.00	1290	-1938.82	3228.821	1290
10.00	1080	-1915.39	2995.39	1080
11.00	1350	-1891.96	3241.959	1350
12.00	1300	-1868.53	3168.528	1300
13.00	1280	-1845.1	3125.097	1280
14.00	1350	-1821.67	3171.666	1350
15.00	1440	-1798.24	3238.235	1440
16.00	1310	-1774.8	3084.804	1310
17.00	1380	-1751.37	3131.373	1380
18.00	1340	-1727.94	3067.942	1340

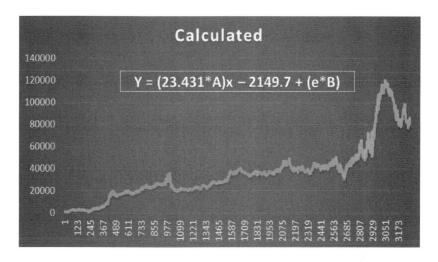

The chart above shows the constructed equity curve using the formula and noise values. It should be obvious that the equity chart looks exactly the same. Remember the point of being able to reconstruct the equity curve was so that we could individually adjust the slope and noise levels. This is what the formula above the equity curve does. You will notice two new elements in the formula A and B. A and B will be used to increase the slope and noise to the desired level. As the value increases for A the slope of the equity curve will increase. Also, to increase the noise level you increase the value of B. By increasing and decreasing A and B it will allow us to see their relationship and effect they have on different systems.

The charts below demonstrate different levels of noise and slope. The blue equity curve is the original equity curve. The orange equity curve will be the new adjusted equity curve. I have also added a moving average to both of the equity curves so that we can compare the performance.

In the first chart below the slope was multiplied by 10 and the noise level was kept the same. You can see that it looks like the equity curve was just rotated. The one thing you may also notice is that the moving average does not break the equity curve as often. Trend following under performs when you have a lack of follow through and this can be shown by how often the equity curve breaks the moving average.

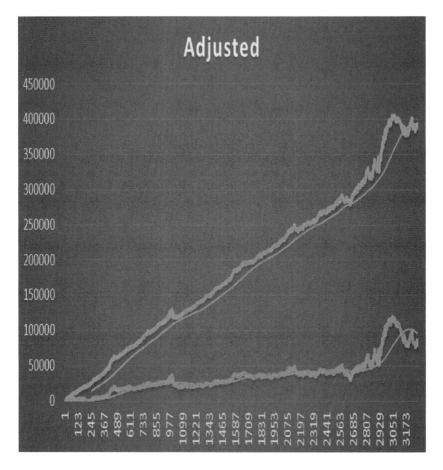

For another comparison in the next chart I left the noise at the same level but this time I multiplied the slope by 20. Again you can see how the increased slope has affected the performance of trend following. This time the moving average is never broken by the equity curve. From these 2 charts there does appear to be a string relationship between system performance, slope and noise.

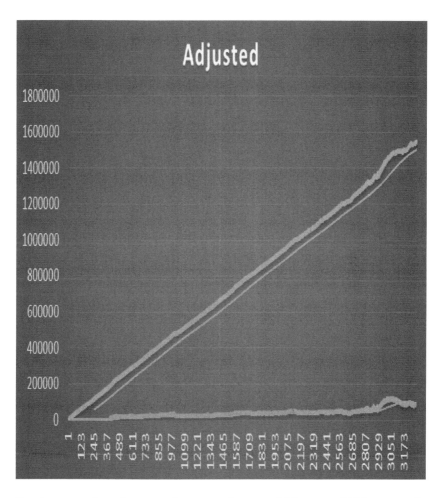

On the next chart I wanted to see what would happen if I increased the noise but left the slope at the same level. The yellow equity curve below shows what happens when you multiply the noise by 10 and leave the slope at the same level. You can really see that the increased noise level has hindered the performance of the trend following system. The equity curve has continually moved back and forth over the moving average. This furthers the point that there is a relationship between the ratio of slope and noise and the performance of trend following.

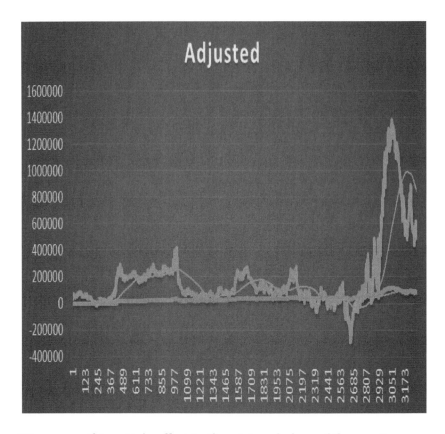

We can see this ratio's affect in the picture below of the equity curve of crude oil. You can see the two different phases on the chart. The first phase is between 2007 and 2008. This phase of the equity curve had a very steep slope with very little noise. It is then obvious if we look at the performance of some trend following CTAs that this would be one of their better periods. The next phase is just the opposite. Between 2009 till now the crude market has had very little slope with a high level of noise. Again if we look at some CTA data we can see that this period has been a struggle for trend following CTAs. When area that has performed during this phase was mean reversion and option selling, these two strategies rely on the market reverting back to the mean.

Speakers of Traders World Online Expo #14

The illustration below summarizes what we have understood up to this point. The formula for the performance of trading following would be P = m/e. Which means that the performance is equal to the slope divided by the noise level. It would be opposite for the performance of mean reversion. It would instead be the noise level divided by the slope. If you think about the reward to risk ratio of each of the systems it makes sense. As the slope increases to infinite and the noise to 0 the trend follower would have an infinite profit. On the other side, if the slope was 0 and the noise level was 12 or any number the trend followers profit would be 0 because there was no increase in the market.

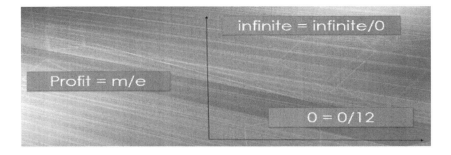

A very robust way of calculating the ratio of noise to slope is to divide the rise or fall in the market by the total distance travelled. The time period is counted as 1 so that the slope will then be just the change in price for that period. Therefore, if the market went up 10 points the slope will be 10. The noise will be the distance travelled back and forth for the market to make the 10 point gain. The two tables below show how to calculate the total distance walked to get to the final point on the equity curve. All you need to do is find the absolute value of the noise and then total up the abs of all the noise. If the equity curve ran directly on the trendline the ratio would be 1. This would represent a straight line to the equity curve. The first table on the left had a slope multiplied by 20 and the table on the right had a noise multiplied by 20.

The chart and table below summarizes the finds for the robust formula. In the table you will see the multiplier for both slope and noise. You will also find the ratio between slope and noise and the performance ratio. As you can see, as the slope multiple increases, so does the performance ratio. Also as the noise increases the performance ratio goes down. The chart also displays that there is a strong relationship between noise, slope and trend following performance.

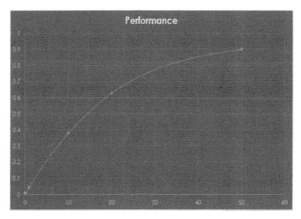

One interesting point of this study that came out was that the trend following filter produced an equity with a lower slope with higher noise than the original market. Option selling was the opposite; it produced an equity curve with a high slope to noise ratio. This would explain why you cannot apply a trend filter to a trend following equity curve. Another interesting point is that the ratio is constantly swinging back and forth as the market cycles through different phases. It also helps explain diversification and displays why you would want to be diversified over time frame and system type.

For more information contact Brady Preston, bradypreston@gmail.com, http://prestoncapllc.com

World Cup Trading Championship: History and the Advantages of Competing by Chad Robbins and Mark Ayoub

Presented by Chad Robbins, Director of Business Development, WorldCupAdvisor.com; and Mark Ayoub, Automated Trading Systems Developer, Addwins LLC.

Chad Robbins:

The World Cup program is built on two pillars: the World Cup Trading Championships® and WorldCupAdvisor.com Leader-Follower AutoTrade™ service.

The World Cup Championship of Futures Trading is a year-long competition. People compete because it's easy to enter, fun to participate, potentially rewarding and the ultimate way to test their skills and earn the respect of the trading community.

Traders fund accounts with a minimum of $10,000 and use their own strategies to post the highest net return by the end of the calendar year. Some day-trade, while others hold positions for weeks or months. Competitors can trade underlying contracts, options or spreads, and use discretionary methods or computerized programs. The public can watch traders jockeying for positions on a daily-updated World Cup leader board at www.worldcupchampionships.com.

There is no entry fee, and each entrant pays a standardized, competitive commission rate. As per the Official Rules, traders can enter at any time during the year but must make a minimum of 10 round-turn trades of any quantity to qualify for awards and prizes.

Prizes include magnificent pewter and crystal Bull & Bear trophies for the Top Three finishers, which are presented at an awards ceremony hosted by the CME Group® on the trading floor. Other outstanding prizes are from such leading vendors as Ninja Trader, Online Trading Academy, Trade Navigator and Finege Trading Computers and WorldCupAdvisor.com. But potentially, the most lucrative prize is the possibility to earn an advisory role on WorldCupAdvisor.com.

WorldCupAdvisor.com offers leader-follower trading programs in which talented professionals from around the world fund their own accounts and display their live futures and forex trading accounts. Subscribers can automatically mirror the trading activity of any WCA lead trader with World Cup AutoTrade service. Lead traders compete with each other to earn customer trust and subscription business.

Subscribers have access to a real-time display of activity in the lead account(s) to which they are subscribed. Each program is supported by separate display screens for orders entered, open positions, closed positions and advisor commentary. When followers are logged into the WCA site, an instant message will appear on the screen and a bell will ring every time there is new activity. An email notification also accompanies each new activity, and subscribers can also receive free text message notifications if desired.

Many WCA advisors have posted top finishes in the World Cup Trading Championships. Other accounts are traded by noted system developers, authors, commentators and educators.

A WorldCupAdvisor.com account is an excellent way to diversify a trading portfolio, regardless of an investor's level of experience. The wide variety of WCA accounts provides opportunity to diversify across asset classes, trading products and strategies. However, diversification in not necessarily available when trading a single program. Prospective followers should evaluate each program's specifications to determine whether or not it is suitable for their diversification requirements.

To help investors determine which WCA programs are right fit for their needs, WCA provides several free online tools to help them make informed decisions. Chief among these is the Net-Profit Calculator, which offers a real-time summary of net performance inclusive of commissions and subscription fees. The NPC displays net profit, return on investment, drawdown, trade volume and more.

WCA also produces detailed Performance Reports for programs with at least three months of trade activity. These month-end reports cover VAMI and stress testing vs. S&P 500, Sharpe and Sortino ratios, distribution of monthly returns, standard deviation and much more. The newest asset is the Personal Portfolio Builder tool, which allows investors to combine performance reports of two or more programs for a look at hypothetical results. Users can vary the start dates and funding levels to find the best match for their needs. Another cornerstone of performance analysis is the closed-trade history provided for every account. This is a grid that shows gross profit and loss for each trade, with buy and sell prices included.

Program subscriptions are sold on a month-to-month basis, eliminating long-term commitments. With AutoTrade service, subscribers can start a new program or stop an existing one with a single phone call to their broker. They can control their own leverage by adjusting funding levels and adding or reducing exposure. AutoTrade service is designed to deliver same-price fills for leader and followers alike; authorized brokers will waive commissions on any WCA leader-follower trade in which a follower's fill price is not equal to or better than the lead trader's fill price (with the exception of trades placed outside a program's AutoTrade block when synchronizing positions for a follower entering a program or liquidating positions for a follower exiting a program).

It is important to emphasize that trading futures and forex involves significant risk of loss and is not suitable for everyone, and that past performance is not necessarily indicative of future results. Following any WCA lead account should be undertaken with risk capital only. Before investing, you should carefully consider your risk tolerance and suitability for this type of investment.

For more information, email info@worldcupadvisor.com or call 1-312-454-5000 or
1-877-456-7111.

Mark Ayoub:

I started day trading penny stocks in 1999 and did well with it making consistent profits. At that time - during the tech stock boom - it was a great time to get started. A couple of years later the tech-stock bubble burst. After that the "pattern day trader rule" was implemented, and so the liquidity in that market really dried up (at least compared to what it was) and so I went on to do other things at that time.

Fast-forward to early 2004 ... I began trading futures and forex. Now when I saw how absolutely easy it was going to be (I say that jokingly because that's what I thought at that time) and when I found out that I could actually automate my trading I thought, "Yep, I'm going to have a money-making machine in two weeks!"

Well it was more like three years and literally, a couple of thousand hours of trial and error until I developed good, working systems that have made consistent profits. And I am glad I did - by 2008, I started placing my systems with brokerages in Chicago (and then elsewhere) and I've been trading automated ever since.

My goal is simple: I want to continue to make profitable systems for myself and make them available to others for trading. I use automated trading systems to accomplish this goal because of several reasons:

A computer has the ultimate trading discipline. As a discretionary trader I've been successful and I've also made probably every mistake that most traders make. Moving stops, targets, letting winners become losers, getting out and back in, etc. I was very business-minded and driven and this can actually work against you as a trader. Those wonderful strengths become weaknesses as you realize that there is no controlling the market and trades. It can be extremely frustrating and cause financial loss. Whereas, a computer can follow the plan flawlessly – so long as it is a good plan! Following a bad plan consistently obviously won't work, and that is the flaw with most automated trading systems out there.

I prefer 24-hour-a-day trading. A computer can watch the charts and wait for a trade setup 24 hours a day. In fact, some of my programs monitor several charts at the same time in order to see a broader picture of the market in order to make improved trading decisions.

Automation eliminates emotional trading. Many brokers experience the same emotional and psychological pitfalls that traders do. As an investor handing money to a broker or CTA to manually trade, what many people forget is that person is human like anyone else, and often times falls into the exact same pitfalls that I just mentioned.

The charts all look different when the market is closed. This is the ultimate "woulda, shoulda, coulda." You look at the chart after a losing day and say, "look what I woulda, shoulda, coulda done… look how easy it is! I'm going to try again tomorrow" and you have another losing day.

Automated trading can be based on years of back-testing. A methodology can be back-tested on years of data and a computer will stick to the plan, which is a good thing - but only if the plan is a winning plan.

A computer will stick to the plan. The markets change constantly and although there are patterns, there is also a randomness to it. A good system can adapt to those changes. Oftentimes, people see a pattern that "works" over and over again and by the time they begin to trade it, things are changing and the discretionary trader tends to want to be "safe" and stick to what they saw work before but now the market is behaving differently. This ironically is one of the major pitfalls to computerized trading as well – it is called, "curve fitting" or "form fitting." For example, developing a system that would only work on a certain market condition, let's say from May 2012 to August 2012 (four months), so as long as that market condition would remain the same, the system would work but as soon as it starts changing the system breaks down.

A good system can adapt to changes in real-time. If the chart would keep repeating those four months of patterns over and over again, you'd have the ultimate system. Again, although I'm not saying that automated trading is flawless, a good system can adapt to changes in real-time and may be able to limit the downside while making relatively consistent profits.

My trading philosophy is simple; its highest priority is capital preservation followed by profits while maintaining a planned and calculated approach.

Many people approach trading with no plan and have not really thought about the downside risk at all. The prevailing thought is, "How much money can I make" or "If I can get one big trade I'm set." While it is possible to get lucky with that one big trade, this approach can be a disaster. People tend to overleverage or hang on to a winning trade until it becomes a loser, and then could end up "revenge trading," which is making stupid knee-jerk decisions to "get their money back that the market took from them." That can lead to other irrational behavior. Trading with the right system, and allowing enough capital for reasonable losses and drawdowns, is a key factor.

While some of what I just mentioned wouldn't apply in automated trading because a good system will attempt to limit those drawdowns and losses, it is still up to the investor to not overleverage to the point where a few losses will be a problem.

Although past hypothetical or even live performance is never a guarantee of the future, an automated system can give you an idea of what to expect as far as risk and profits are concerned and this is important - all of this helps the investor or trader go into it with a plan.

Most traders (I think it is around 90%) lose money in the markets. A lot of it is for the reasons we've already discussed: Emotion, fear, no plan, etc.

But also, there are many automated systems out there that are junk - they simply don't work. So when I talk about the strengths of automation I am making the assumption that it is a robust system that has the potential to work in real-time with real money and make real profits.

My Addwins Euro FX system has the following components:

Trades Euro FX Futures (CME)

Breakout system

Looks for sharp moves in the market

Trades both long and short

Targets and Stops are dynamic but there is a maximum

Daytrade System (out by 4:30pm CST)

Please remember that trading futures and forex involves significant risk of loss and is not suitable for everyone. Past performance is not necessarily indicative of future results.

"Edwards Angles" New Paradigm Pitchfork Trading by Byran Edwards

Stop right here if you want to learn why price just turns around seemingly for no reason and heads in the opposite direction! Sometimes it reaches just out beyond the previous swing high or low and then turns just as you entered the pro trend trade. If you have ever wondered how or why this article was written for you.

Pitchforks, aka Median sets, or Edwards Angles date back to the 1900's and Roger Babson with the "Normal Line" principle which Alan Andrews developed into the "Pitchfork." I, with the help of my trading team and mentor Steve Gregor developed what I now call Edwards Angles. It is a combination of everything Newton, Babson and Andrews discovered and taught but with real time, leading indicator use and often are the exact support or resistance lines price wicked out to touch right before going back to hit your old paradigm stop loss. Edwards Angles with the help of Harmonic Wave Convergence can help you know when to sell instead of buy and buy instead of sell.

Welcome to the New Paradigm, you have a choice now to continue into a new way of thinking and possibly a complete shift in the way you view the markets and definitely Pitchforks and choose success over the same old same old. Or, you can pretend you didn't see this intro and go back to the old paradigm where the stoplosses are huge, the money management is random, the Support and Resistance doesn't have any rhyme or reason and price movement seems unexplainable.

Harmonic Wave Convergence is a topic of its own, presented in another section and for the sake of time cannot be explained here, but uses "MultiWave" which is a wave measurement tool that measures the wave strength of up to 7 different time frames and plots them on **one** chart. It uses the Elliot Wave principle that a longer term wave cannot terminate until the lower level wave beneath it terminates at the same time, and the lower level wave beneath that, etc. Great news though, you DO NOT have to trade Elliott Wave, like it, count it, or even understand it to trade.

MultiWave with Edwards Angles on MotiveWave Charts!

It is possible to watch the Waves of 1 minute, 3 minute, 5 minute, 10 minute, 30 minute, 60 minute and 4 hour charts all on one chart with your Edwards Angles drawn on it and know the precise moment all 7 waves terminate, often on a to-the-pip-tag of one of our Pitchforks. Like in the examples in the video module part of Traders World Online Expo #14.

So other than combined use with MultiWave what makes Edwards Angles so special? Great question! It is the mindset that I teach, the concepts of using "A" swing high, "A" swing low and "A" previous swing low, not "The" as in there is only one correct option for your Pitchforks to be drawn. I teach draw, draw and redraw. Practice makes perfect, but only if you are practicing the correct way. If you are doing it incorrectly over and over then you have just gotten real good at doing it wrong. There are very precise rules for drawing Pitchforks, the direction they point and some great guidelines for selection of the Swing Highs and Lows you connect the Pitchfork to.

The highlight of Edwards Angles is also my favorite Pitchfork. Andrews called it a Traditional set. It is that, with the rules for where and how to draw them, but with the addition of MultiWave on your charts they become "Predictive!" Yes, even a forecast of sorts. It, like most things in technical trading isn't a guarantee of a winning trade, but it is one more thing in your favor, and the more things in your favor the better your chances of succeeding. The

Predictive Pitchfork uses set points in chart history. 3 points in history, usually swing highs and lows connected by the fork and then pointed to the right on the chart. Then literally we just wait for price to come to one of our stationary lines and bounce on it while at the same time we have the phenomenon of Harmonic Wave Convergence on our charts and up to 7 different waves terminating at the same time as we get in with sometime 3-5 pip stoploss. If there is no Convergence but price hits one of the Pitchforks, sometimes that is still a trade, but for the advanced trader and covered more in depth in the PipClub full day classes. The opposite it true, but more often. If there is Convergence of MultiWave, ShredderFX traders have other ways of knowing when to take the trade beyond the Pitchforks, also covered more in depth in the full day classes.

There are other types of Edwards Angles to draw and the same principle is used when there is a convergence and a resulting trade. They are the Schiff, Modified Schiff and Traditional. So there are Pitchforks to fit any chart, any time frame, any schedule, any lifestyle and most importantly any currency pair. (Any market for that matter, I just trade Forex.) In most strategies that is not the case, the large majority of them I have looked at have some parameters like they work best on the Euro, best in the Asian session, or are best for daily position traders. Edwards Angles powered by MultiWave works for everyone: the "scalper" on a 1 minute chart, the busy professional who can trade a few times a week and respond to an alert, and of course those with flexibility to trade anything anytime.

So why Median sets? Why am I here talking about them instead of MACD, a magic EMA cross or the latest and greatest trading app for your Smartphone or tablet? It is really quite simple. I have traded it, successfully. Have you ever been sold something that someone doesn't believe in or even use themselves? I have and you can tell. I believe in this system, the Pitchforks, the MultiWave and the newest addition to the ShredderFX program MotiveWave Charts and have had success with it and that experience has given me insight into price movement, more confidence, less stress and more trades with higher profit.

While they do contain channel price history, median sets are evaluated against current price action, thus in reality, are "real time" trading tools they are not a lagging indicator. Median sets have precise turn-around zones, therefore small stops can be used. Intra-day trading and short-term trading and thus fit extremely well within the ShredderFX Money Management System. Yes, money management, not something many traders want to talk about or are even taught today in most programs, with our tight stops comes increased lot sizes, and more profit per pip but all the while never risking more than 2% of our account.

Because of their consistency, Pitchforks can be traded fairly objectively, thus complimenting (not destroying) the trader's psychological growth. I, like some of you got eaten alive when I first started trading. Margin calls, drained live accounts and a resulting complete lack of confidence in myself and trading in general. I was taught properly how to trade, how not to get margined out and to trade demo for as long as it took before ever investing a dime of my real money! Did I listen? Not to all of it. After about 2 years I had enough and went looking for more, and that is when I found Steve Gregor and the ShredderFX system with PipClub. Here I began to gain my confidence back and saw a system that was objective and not subjective. If price hit the Median Set and we had Harmonic Wave Convergence we took the trade, if not we didn't. It was/is rules based and it either was a trade or it wasn't. I began to draw Pitchforks everyday (I post some of them on twitter @bryanpipslam) and quickly got my confidence back and psychologically began to grow and change into the successful trader I am today.

I could sing the praises of the Pitchfork all day but just have a few more positives I must point out. Median sets are drawn and analyzed in the candlestick area, thus take up no additional real-estate on the trader's charts. This was huge for me! What good is a chart with so many indicators and mark ups on it if you can't see it? They work very streamline with any chart platform and make the charts easier to read, not harder. The lines are mostly diagonal, with the occasional Pitchfork that is almost flat, they all have some slope therefore they add a "time factor" not available with horizontal support and resistance. The Pitchforks intersect with moving averages, Fibonacci's and other S&R on your chart showing one specific moment in time where there is great potential for reversal. We call these areas PRZ's for potential reversal zones.

Edwards Angles are relatively easy to learn to draw and analyze (compared to other advanced studies) and have much more "data" compared to typical trend lines. In fact we sometimes refer to the Pitchfork as the lazy man's trendline. That Predictive Pitchfork we talked about earlier usually ends up with one of the parallel lines looking like a trendline, but drawn before the touches. Often times the Pitchforks surround the ShredderFX's 62 (center of the road) EMA increasing probability of successful proven money management and trade entry.

So there you have it. Edwards Angles are very simply Median Sets/Pitchforks drawn with very specific, easy to learn rules and guidelines. Along side them we have MultiWave and almost a fool proof system for the complete trader development program. Money Management, Personal and Psychological growth, real time indicators, application to any timeframe in any market suitable for any lifestyle with a proven track record of success in winning trades and hundreds of impacted traders surrounding the globe. Won't you come a join us in the New Paradigm? There is plenty of room and we will be there every step of the way if you have any questions along your journey to Jedi Trader Status!

Contact Bryan Edwards at bryanedwards@pipclub.com

OTHER KINDLE BOOKS

Gann Masters Course

Gann-Trade Real Time

Speakers of Traders World Online Expo #14

Gann Master Charts Unveiled

Patterns & Ellipses

Best Trading Strategies

A Unique Approach to Forecasting

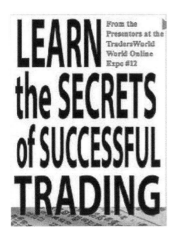

Learn the Secrets of Successful Trading

Speakers of Traders World Online Expo #14

Finding Your Trading Method

DAY TRADING TURMOIL TO TRIUMPH

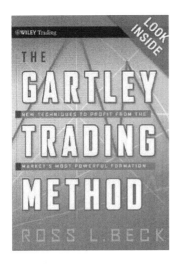

The Gartley Trading Method: New Techniques to Profit From the Market's Most Powerful Formation

Traders World Digest #1 thru #27

Speakers of Traders World Online Expo #14

ON DEMAND VIDEOS FROM THE TRADERS WORLD ONLINE EXPO EXPIRES DECEMBER 31ST, 2013

You can now play the Traders World Online Expo #14 video presentations directly from your Kindle fire, HD, HDX, Nook, Ipad, Iphone, Android Tablet or computer. Get access by going to http://www.tradersworldonlineexpo.com and by clicking the line entries below on the site. (You must have internet access and compatible device for this to work).

1. Adrienne Togharie - Fear of Trading
2. Steven Primo - The Right Way To Trade Tops and Bottoms
3. Steve Wheeler - Trades That Work...(So You Don't Have To)
4. Bill Dennis - Cutting Edge News & Social Media Analytics
5. George Krum - TA Tools for Mobile Devices
6. Hawk Arps - Identifying Trading Pullbacks in a Trend
7. Thomas Barmann - Algorithmic Trading with Human Interaction
8. Mike Barna - How the TSL Machine Designed the #1 rated Futures Truth Strategy
9. Gail Mercer - Using Volume Analysis to Easily Identify Low Risk Opportunities
10. Troy Epperson - Trading Methods you can Profit from Immediately
11. Gabriel Brent - APA Zones exposing the hidden order flow
12. Scott Andrews - 5 Ways to Determine Where a Market Will Close
13. Al McWhirr - A brief review of all EminiScalp trading methods, with the focus being on our LTD, PLUS, ATA and EminiScalp Intervals.
14. Robert Miner - Time and Price Targets for Support/Resistance and Trend Reversal
15. Jack Crooks - Seeing market in three-waves and trading the C!

16. Jan Arps - The Trend Can Be Your Very Good Friend
17. Larry Gaines - 5 Powerful Trading Essentials" every trader must know for swing trades & day trades
18. Ken Chow - How to Pick Highs and Lows Accurately
19. Tom Alexander - The Market Profile Graph and Auction Market Concepts
20. Ross Givens - The Perfect Growth Stock
21. Brady Preston - Slope and Noise - Relationship to Profit
21. Lars Von Thienen - Combining Cyclic Analysis with Genetic Algorithms
22. Brady Preston - Slope and Noise - Relationship to Profit
23. Gerard P. Reynaud - The Simplest Proven Day Trading Method with a Track Record
24. John Matteson - The 4-Step Trading Process
25. Rande Howell - Overcoming Self Sabotage to Become a Consistently Profitable Trader
26. Saul Shaoul - Learn to Scalp the Market Daily - Live Online from the Trading Pits in Chicago
27. Eloy - Fenocchi - A Simple Edge for Active Traders
28. John Karnas - Addressing the Trend Trading Challenge of Monitoring Many Markets and Only Trading the Ones That Are Trending - ALL on 1 Monitor!
29. Mark Ayoub & Chad Robbins -World Cup Trading Championship, History and the Advantages of Competing
30. Ross L. Beck - How to Trade Gartley Patterns
31. Steve Gregor - Harmonic Wave Convergence - The New Paradigm of Currency Trading

After December 31, 2013 you can only access these videos as well as hundreds of videos from prior Traders World Online Expo and all 55 back issues of Traders World Magazine. Reg. $39.95 Now only $19.95 save 50%. 60-day money back guarantee. Click here to be a TradersWorld Premium Subscriber

Speakers of Traders World Online Expo #14

COPYRIGHT

Copyright 2013 Halliker's, Inc. All rights reserved. Information in this publication must not be reproduced in any form without written permission from the publisher. Traders World Digest is published quarterly by Halliker's, Inc., 2508 W. Grayrock Dr., Springfield, MO 65810. Created in the U.S.A. is prepared from information believed to be reliable but not guaranteed us without further verification and does not purport to be complete.

ISBN-13:
978-1493799572

DISCLAIMER

This material is intended for educational purposes only and is believed to be accurate, but its accuracy is not guaranteed. Trading and investing has large potential rewards and large potential risks. You must be aware of, and fully understand these risks and be willing to accept them in order to invest in equity, futures, options, currencies and other financial markets. Do not trade with money that you cannot afford to lose. No representation is being made that any account will or is likely to achieve profits or losses similar to those discussed. The past performance of any trading system or methodology is not necessarily indicative of future results.

Investing and Trading involve significant financial risk and is not suitable for everyone. No communication should be considered as financial or trading advice. All information is intended for educational purposes only.

You will need to do your own due diligence and perform your own research.

There are substantial risks of loss when trading any market. Please read the NFA's and other agencies' disclosures and fully understand your risks.

Futures and options trading are speculative and involves risk of loss. Opinions expressed are subject to revision without further notification. We are not offering to buy or sell securities or commodities discussed. Halliker's Inc., one or more of its officers, and/or authors may have a position in the securities or commodities discussed herein. Any article that shows hypothetical or stimulated performance results have certain inherent limitations, unlike an actual performance record; simulated results do not represent actual trading. Also, since the trades have not already been executed, the results may have under - or over compensated for the impact, if any, of certain market factors, such as lack of liquidity. Simulated trading programs in general are also subject to the fact that they are designated with the benefits of hindsight. No representation is being made that any account will or is likely to achieve profits or losses similar to those shown. The names of products and services presented in this magazine are used only in editorial fashion and to the benefit of the trademark owner with no intention of infringing on trademark rights.

CFTC RULE 4.41 - HYPOTHETICAL OR SIMULATED PERFORMANCE RESULTS HAVE CERTAIN LIMITATIONS. UNLIKE AN ACTUAL PERFORMANCE RECORD, SIMULATED RESULTS DO NOT REPRESENT ACTUAL TRADING. ALSO, SINCE THE TRADES HAVE NOT BEEN EXECUTED, THE RESULTS MAY HAVE UNDER-OR-OVER COMPENSATED FOR THE IMPACT, IF ANY, OF CERTAIN MARKET FACTORS, SUCH AS LACK OF LIQUIDITY. SIMULATED TRADING PROGRAMS IN GENERAL ARE ALSO SUBJECT TO THE FACT THAT THEY ARE DESIGNED WITH THE BENEFIT OF HINDSIGHT. NO REPRESENTATION IS BEING MADE THAT ANY ACCOUNT WILL OR IS LIKELY TO ACHIEVE PROFIT OR LOSSES SIMILAR TO THOSE SHOWN.

Printed in Great Britain
by Amazon.co.uk, Ltd.,
Marston Gate.